The
Perfect
Rehearsal

IT'S A TRIP!

by Timothy Seelig

Layout/Design: Shawn Northcutt
Photography: Shawn Northcutt
Cover Design: Joe Rattan

Shawnee Press, Inc.
1221 17th Avenue South • Nashville, TN 37212

TABLE OF CONTENTS

i

Part Two: Hitting the Road
Rehearsals begin

ACKNOWLEDGEMENTS

For fear of sounding like the "not-so-shocked" winner at a televised awards ceremony who pulls out a three-page list of thank you's, I do have a little something prepared.

There are many people to thank for helping me get to this point, but I'll try to narrow it down.

I want to thank:

1. Every person who ever conducted a rehearsal in which I was a singer or player.

Actually, I owe them a thank you and an apology. We conductors (and future conductors) make the worst choir members of all. We are always the ones cutting up in the back of the room, most often with a completely straight face. For that, I am sorry. Take comfort in the fact that I am being repaid every week with a room full of choir, band, and orchestra conductors who sing in my chorus!

2. Every person who ever sat through a rehearsal I conducted.

You taught me everything I know. You patiently helped sandpaper the rough edges of my conducting and my life. Thank you to the men and the women who, through these many years, laughed at my jokes (over and over) and allowed me to use them as guinea pigs as I learned how to be a conductor.

3. The 250 men of the Turtle Creek Chorale.

You have shown up week after week for 20 years. You literally helped me grow up – in every way possible. Your loyalty and artistry are, and will continue to be, a source of inspiration to me and to many others around the world.

4. The people who have believed in me over these many years.

Mom and Dad, of course. My two children, Judson and Corianna, who either sat in the back of many rehearsals or stayed home while Dad did his thing. My other family, friends, and partner Shawn, whose patience rivals that of Mother Teresa.

5. My friends at Shawnee Press.

For some reason, these wonderful folks believed you would like to read my books (if not my mind). Thanks to Greg, Mark, Anissa, Krista, Joseph, and crew.

6. My colleagues in GALA, ACDA, and Chorus America.

Certainly I have learned more from my fellow conductors in these three great organizations than in my formal education. Watching you, listening to your choruses, attending conventions and festivals has been the true lifeblood of this career. This certainly includes all who sent me their thoughts about what rehearsals mean to them.

7. My proofreaders.

Once again, thanks to the folks who agreed to help me limit the boo-boo's and make your reading more pleasurable. Thanks, Kenn, Mark, Robert, and Sandy! And most especially Gary for reading it over and over.

8. Dr. Jo-Michael Scheibe

My friend and colleague who, from his vast experience and fresh perspective, provided a bonus chapter in this book. It is priceless and provides a completely different point of view. Thank you for sharing your wisdom so selflessly.

9. Special contributors

All the conductors, singers, and friends who have added their thoughts to "What others think about a perfect rehearsal." I know it was a difficult assignment and I appreciate, more than you can know, your time, energy, and willingness to share your thoughts. Special thanks to the two outside "reviewers" who wrote about rehearsals.

PART ONE: PLANNING THE TRIP
Before the First Rehearsal

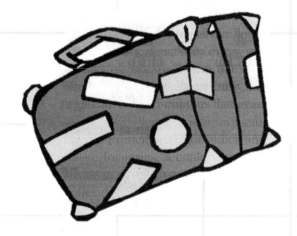

Why Are You Embarking on This Choral Journey?

What Kind of Conductor/Tour Guide Are You?

Selecting the Destination

Who Will Help You Along the Way?

Mapping Out the Trip/Rehearsals

Packing for the Trip – Physically and Emotionally

How Long Will It Take to Get There?

Recruitment and Motivation

INTRODUCTION
The Perfect Rehearsal ... It's a Trip!

When first asked to write a book called *The Perfect Rehearsal*, I was not sure what in the world I would write. Certainly I have spent thousands and thousands of hours in rehearsals – both orchestra and chorus. Like you, I know something about rehearsals or I wouldn't still be doing this after more than 30 years. Everything was simply intuitive, not something I had studied. When challenged to write down what it really takes to pull off a successful rehearsal, I was amazed at how difficult it was. For many, it comes naturally; for some it is not that simple. In most cases, our rehearsals are run like the ones we grew up experiencing. That may not be the best we can do.

In *The Perfect Blend*, I combined two of my favorite pastimes as the overriding analogy for the book: food and music. Rehearsals have very little to do with food (too little, in my opinion). It became immediately obvious that this book should involve another of my passions – travel. Everything about rehearsals is mirrored in taking a wonderful journey. So, hang on to your seats and enjoy the ride.

Rehearsing is unlike most trips since most of the time is spent en route rather than at the destination. You would never spend 50 hours traveling just to spend two hours and then start back.

TAKE NOTE!

Before you plan another concert,
Before you choose one piece of music,
Before you invite singers to come along,
READ THIS BOOK!
It may change the entire journey.

2

This journey began with writing *The Perfect Blend.*

I never imagined that I would write a book. Well, that is not true. We all fantasize about writing our life story and it becoming a best-seller. Then we move to the next step: decide who will play us in the movie – a huge blockbuster just waiting to happen. Playing the part of Tim Seelig was to be, of course, Tom Cruise. Then he jumped on that couch on the Oprah Show. Back to the drawing board. His loss.

The title, *The Perfect Blend,* was chosen because it reflected the wide variety of information the book contained. It is a mixture of all kinds of things that will hopefully lead one to a perfect blend of technique, and the perfect rehearsal and performance. The major emphasis is on vocal and choral technique and vocal health. A few places in this book will overlap since good vocal and choral technique are taught in rehearsals. You need to have both books on your shelf.

The Perfect Rehearsal? Is it just Fantasy Island? Maybe.

I have heard from many of my colleagues that in their experience, there is no such thing. A perfect rehearsal would be one where the conductor was completely prepared, feeling great, on task and organized, ready to give and receive. It is also one where every singer in the room would show up completely prepared, feeling great, hydrated and focused, and ready to absorb every pearl of wisdom offered by the conductor.

In addition, the room would be the perfect temperature, the lighting just right, enough space for the singers to feel comfortable, and no interruptions whatsoever. Every task would be accomplished and more. Love would permeate every last acoustical tile in the ceiling. (Oh, never mind, there are no acoustical tiles in the perfect rehearsal.) I don't know why that seems so out of the ordinary. It happens for me every rehearsal. OK, almost every rehearsal? OK, I remember one – in my dreams!

Maybe there is no such thing as a perfect rehearsal, much like there is really no perfect performance (ouch, that hurt). There can't be a perfect performance for several reasons: we are humans, we work with humans, and regardless of how flawless we think it might be, the definition of perfect is still quite subjective. The truly perfect performances obviously all took place prior to the invention of recording devices.

What other perfect things do we strive for in life? The perfect spouse, house, pet or child? When we are young, we begin with a long list of attributes we would like in a spouse. As we grow older, more mature and perhaps a bit jaded, the list narrows from "gorgeous, talented, brilliant and rich," to simply "breathing." Surely we have not gone that far in our hopes for rehearsals! Is the perfect rehearsal just a fantasy? Maybe. But who wants to live life with no dreams and few fantasies?

With this in mind, we launch into the task of making our rehearsals as perfect as we possibly can. The task is daunting, but without daunting tasks, what is the point, the excitement, the goal?

Question: What is the most important thing you do as a choral conductor?

Some would argue that it is the selection of repertoire; some, the preparation of that repertoire. There are many who think the most important thing you do is keep good records (i.e., administrators). Others value fund-raising expertise, public persona, and cooperation with administration or boards. Then there are those for whom "jazz hands" are the ultimate. Truly, all of these are important, except maybe "jazz hands." Balance in all things is the key, but the bottom line is a successful rehearsal technique.

Answer: Rehearse!

Throughout your career as a conductor, there is never enough time to prepare for rehearsals. In the beginning, you are busy with a million other things: school, family, multiple careers, gigs, etc. This doesn't change much for professional musicians. But when you are young, you feel more invincible than when you get a little older and perhaps wiser. There is more confidence in "winging it." There is a reliance on that "innate musicality" as opposed to the "learned musicianship." This is a dangerous pattern.

Some think the most important thing is the performance. After all, we only hear or read about the performances! Or contests! Or the festivals! We only hear (and talk) about the destination, not the journey. Even tour books focus on the destination, not how much fun you can have in the car, train, plane or boat!

Have you ever read a review of a rehearsal in the local paper? Much (perhaps too much) has been written about choral performances. And much has been written about conductors of those performances as well. But who is writing about the rehearsals? After all, this is where it all happens! Our papers have endless coverage of training camps for every possible sport. They talk about the players who make up the team. They talk about what they are eating, what they are wearing, what they are saying. They talk about the coach. How is he running things? What does he think about the players and the team, etc. They interview the players and everyone who is in the stands just to watch the rehearsals. Oops, I mean practices.

But the same thing does not happen in what we do. They only care about the performance. The reality is, most of the sports media has a good idea during training camp what the team is going to be like. So should we. Perhaps the music critics should somehow turn the clock back and become a fly on the wall at our "training camp." Most likely, they would be able to tell what the performance was going to be like by observing rehearsals. For that reason, I have included two outsider's "reviews" of a rehearsal in the final chapter.

TAKE NOTE!

Boring rehearsals = Boring performances
Exciting rehearsals = Exciting performances
Creative rehearsals = Creative performances
Engaged singers = Engaged audiences

Many books on choral music provide you with the tools of the trade required for rehearsal. A list of "How to" resources is in the back of this book. But it doesn't matter how well you plan if your heart is not in it and your mind is not ready for it.

This book will give you some new insights into your own view of the choral rehearsal. It will give you some new tools, but is mostly geared toward "how you feel" about your rehearsals and how your singers feel about them as well. When both of those things are on track, many other issues will automatically clear up. All of a sudden, we, as conductors, will be more fulfilled. Our singers will start being more responsive because of our "homework." More members will be attracted to the group and most importantly, the performances will reflect this new achievement and attitude.

Psychological and emotional preparation for rehearsal is probably more important in the long run than the actual busy work that is required for running an organized rehearsal. Some say the performance is the most important part of a chorus's life. But the rehearsals are what form the absolute core to the art of singing in a group.

What happens in rehearsals provides the real essence of choral singing and is what makes it special and beloved by those who choose to participate in it. It is like no other activity on earth in that regard and makes singing in a choir a team sport instead of just a group of soloists getting together to sing.

At some point, you must have been smitten with the experience of singing in a choir and that experience must have included rapturous choir rehearsals somewhere along the way. If you hated everything about being in a choir, you would never have chosen this profession and therefore would certainly not be reading this book.

Ponder how many hours are spent in rehearsals as compared to performance. Regardless of whether you conduct a choir in a school, church or community setting, the number of hours in rehearsal vs. performance is at least ten hours for every one hour of performance time. For most choruses, 40 hours is a more accurate number.

This is not unlike the training any other athlete (and I do consider us all vocal athletes) might go through. Imagine how many hours it takes for a gymnast to work up a one-minute routine on the balance beam!! Singers have nothing to whine about. What if you worked for 10 or 12 years for one minute on the beam, and then fell off?

Spending years on a one-minute routine is definitely an instance when the act of practice has to be worthwhile, energizing, and fulfilling. As choral singers and conductors, we at least get a routine that lasts an hour or two. We have a great deal to learn from our "athlete" cohorts about patience, persistence, and practice.

I thought it would be interesting to estimate the number of hours spent in rehearsal with just one choir, the Turtle Creek Chorale, in one season.

3 hours every Tuesday x 45 weeks =	*135 hours*
3 hours most Sundays x 30 weeks =	*90 hours*
Dress rehearsals, orchestra rehearsals, etc.	*25 hours*
Rehearsals for small group performances	*20 hours*

TOTAL: 270 hours

This is in rehearsals alone! In one year! This doesn't include the church choirs, college choirs, women's chorus, mixed chorus, small ensembles, etc. that I have conducted in addition to the Chorale. That number would just make us all want to sit down and rest for a bit. It also does not include retreats, preparation for tours, appearances at conventions, festivals, recordings, etc. This is my 20th year, so a modest 5,400 hours have been spent in rehearsal with just one ensemble! I have some members who have been there the entire time with almost perfect attendance. Bless their hearts!

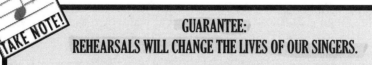

GUARANTEE:
REHEARSALS WILL CHANGE THE LIVES OF OUR SINGERS.

NO GUARANTEE:
PERFORMANCES WILL CHANGE THE LIVES OF OUR AUDIENCE.

Chapter 1

WHY Are You Embarking on This Choral Journey?
Why ARE You Embarking on This Choral Journey?
Why Are YOU Embarking on This Choral Journey?
Why Are You Embarking on THIS Choral Journey?

(Read the above with the appropriate emphasis on the word in ALL caps.)

Are you certain this is a trip you want to take?

Discerning the path to take is one of the most important lessons I have been teaching my university students for the last 20 years. Sometimes we arrive at our chosen destination and don't know how we got there! Perhaps we didn't know where we wanted to go, so someone simply gave us a gentle nudge and hinted that we might consider going in a particular direction. Perhaps it wasn't a gentle nudge at all, but a firm shove. Perhaps we got started in a particular direction and, being stubborn, refused to stop and ask for directions. Perhaps we looked at all of the destinations and decided on this one because someone we knew had chosen it and therefore so did we. But the fact remains that if you are reading this, you are either a conductor of a choir, an orchestra or a band, or you are my Mother.

Few of us choose one path and remain on it for a lifetime. I certainly have not. Indulge me in a brief tale of my own journey. By relating this story, I hope you will be able to see similarities in your own situation.

Entering college in 1969, I was torn between math and music but chose the latter. To be considered the "cream of the crop" of new music students, it was expected that you declare "performance" as your major.

Luckily for us, many young students actually proclaim other majors these days, as far-ranging as music education, vocal pedagogy, music therapy, and even music business. But in the late '60s – before cassette recorders, copiers, or cell phones – we didn't have as many choices.

So, performance it was. And what did that mean? Opera. I had actually seen operas, thanks to my parents, but wouldn't say I was in love with the art form. It was just what you were supposed to say. And I convinced myself thoroughly that singing opera was what I wanted to do.

Time passed. Realizing my voice had to catch up with my body, I just kept going to school and received several (4) degrees: Bachelors Degree in Vocal Performance; Masters Degree in Vocal Performance; Diploma from the Mozarteum in Salzburg, Austria in Vocal Performance; and a DMA in Vocal Performance. (Lucky for me, throughout all those degrees I had studied choral conducting as a minor.) Regardless of how difficult or impossible it seemed, I kept repeating the mantra: "I want to be an opera singer. I want to be an opera singer." No one ever questioned it.

Finally, miracle of miracles, I found the **Holy Grail**! I landed one of the few, elusive jobs as a full-time singer with the Swiss national opera company in a stunning little opera house in the alps outside Zurich! Many people worked hard to help get me there, including my wife and two children, aged one and three at the time, who accompanied me on this adventure. (We didn't really make the kids work.) After years and years of hard work, the goal was achieved. I was an opera singer! (Full-time, no less! And in Europe!)

Once at the destination I had worked toward for so long, I realized, much to my dismay, it was the wrong one! I was singing in a different opera three and four nights a week, worrying about my voice, worrying about my words, my roles, my reviews, and about paying the bills. Every afternoon, rather than play with the kids, rest was the order of the day. Every night I was back on stage. Finally, in a moment of frightening self-examination and honesty, I realized I was not cut out to be an opera singer at all.

At my core, I am a giver, a teacher, a very social being. I need the interaction of others that being on the stage, playing a role, did not afford. No one had ever told me this part: *Perhaps your personality is not compatible with the destination (career) you have chosen.*

The despair was unforgettable. A letter from a friend in the States expressed some life-changing thoughts. "We all have choices in life. You chose a path for yourself that you thought was the right one. You traveled it with all your might and found a dead end awaiting you. So, what are you going to do now? How long are you going to simply sit and stare at that dead end before you backtrack to the last crossroad and take the other path?" It resonated within me and I decided, "Not very long."

Swallowing my pride, and eating crow in spades, we packed up the family and headed home to see what was in store. No one – friends, family or professors – would ever have imagined that what was in store was a career as a choral conductor. That alternative path has been the most rewarding experience of my life. This entire story brings me to some words of advice:

Look deep within and make sure this is a journey you want to continue to make! If you are unhappy and dread every single rehearsal, perhaps you need to look back at the LAST fork in the road.

Now I take every opportunity to ask a few questions of every student who walks through my door:

Question #1
What brought you to the decision to pursue a performance degree?

Question #2
What do you hope to do with that performance degree?

Question #3
Is there anything else you could do in your life that would make you happy?

If the answer to:
Question #1 is
"Because everyone says I sing really well," we pause.

Question #2 is
"Sing opera for a living," we pause.

Question #3 is
"No," we pause even longer.

The same concerns can be voiced with any career decision. If a student says, "I want to be a choral conductor," the same introspection and self-assessment are absolutely warranted.

Don't get me wrong, I wouldn't give anything for the road taken because it made me who I am today. However, with a little more thought given to the compatibility of my chosen career with my personality profile, I could have prepared differently for that career, or prepared better for a variety of options.

Self-assessment

1. Can you identify the moment you knew music would be your life?
2. Can you identify the actual moment you decided to be a conductor?
3. Can you name the person who was leading the group in which you were singing or playing?
4. Have you written them to thank them?
5. Have you been able to recreate some of the magic that person created for you?
6. Have any of your students or singers turned to this as a profession because your love for it was infectious?
7. Are you able to back off from your current position and objectively assess where you are in your own career?
8. Is there something else you could do that could bring you the same satisfaction?
9. How did you get this far?
10. What kinds of extrinsic motivation did you have? (What others wanted.)
11. What types of intrinsic motivation did you experience? (What you wanted.)

If you still want to travel this road after answering these questions, buckle up and let's go.

Chapter 2

What Kind of Conductor/Tour Guide Are You?
Have you renewed your license?

Surely you have driven on a vacation before. But have you ever led a tour? How often have you guided a group to its choral destination? How many were successful? Did you learn lessons from all of them? How often do you have your license renewed? Are you continuing to learn and improve and grow? At what point should your license be revoked?

What kind of driver are you? Clifton Ware, the author of *Basics of Vocal Pedagogy,* describes several styles of teaching. These pertain to conductors as well.

1. **Guru (elitist).** Charismatic, intellectual, aloof, mysterious – exercises authoritarian control over singers. Guru-types rely on cult-like practices to gather and hold "believers" who share and protect the master's "secrets." Singers blindly worship gurus and may become their clones.
2. **Gatekeeper (purist).** Allows only the most serious, dedicated and talented singers to enter his/her domain. Once admitted, the singer is subjected to high standards of performance and rigorous assessment.
3. **Tour guide (populist).** Acts as travel agent who attracts visitors into his/her discipline. Enthusiastically and cheerfully takes singers (and audience) on pleasant excursions highlighting attractive aspects of their discipline. They relate on a personal and informal level and win converts through persuasive means.
4. **Sherpa (guide).** Helps singers master challenges, easing the way. As the singers improve, the sherpa reduces control and encourages singers to assume more responsibility. Conductor/singer relationship is more a partnership

Most people are a combination of the above. Few fit into one category only, although you may know some.

There are basically two kinds of people, both able to have successful careers in music. Knowing which you are helps you work on the skill-set that is not automatic. There are "top-down" thinkers and "bottom-up" thinkers.

The "top-down" thinker can see (or hear) the final product in their mind's eye and/or ear. They may not be as adept at figuring out "how" they are going to get there.

The "bottom-up" thinker gathers all of the building blocks. Once done, they put them together and just hope there is a satisfying whole when assembled.

You, as a choral conductor are required to be both. You are the visionary. You can see the concert, hear the concert, even visualize the audience response before the very first rehearsal. But you are also required to build it from the bottom up: one building block; one singer; one dynamic marking; one piece of music; ONE REHEARSAL at a time.

Top-down thinkers are the people who are truly the geniuses of our time and our field. These are people like Bill and Linda Gates, who visualize an end product and set about figuring out how to get there. The Gates have visualized a world without poverty and disease and are doing all they can to try to help us arrive at this lofty destination. No sitting around thinking "We can never even make a dent, so why try?" Rather than having meeting after meeting to decide what to do next, they have simply taken the first steps and will adjust as they go along.

The bottom-up thinkers have to get all of the building blocks in a room, spread them out on the floor, look at them, sort them, touch them, and hope they add up to a whole. There is a danger in this kind of thinking because there is always the possibility that the sum of the parts is not truly a whole. This is more true of the choral musician than orchestra or band directors. An orchestra conductor gets to choose one symphony for a program. We, on the other hand, must select 15 or more individual building blocks to make a concert.

There are many tools that will help you know more about yourself before taking the first step into the rehearsal room.

If you love the performances but not the rehearsals;
If you love the rehearsals more than the preparation;
If you love the product more than the process;
If you love the end more than the means;
If you live for audience applause, not the gratification of your singers.

TAKE A MOMENT AND ASSESS YOUR OWN PERSONALITY
AS IT FITS INTO YOUR LIFE AND THE OCCUPATION YOU
HAVE CHOSEN.

This exercise is about finding out who you really are as a person. It is to
help you fill in weak areas in your personality profile by learning and honing
the skills of other personality types. This will make you more successful
in what you are doing and, most importantly, more happy. Remember the
old saying, "If Momma's not happy, no one's gonna be happy."

Have you ever been described by a four-letter word?

Have you ever described yourself with one? Let's see, genius has six
letters, brilliant has nine! What four-letter word are you? I am referring
to the four-letter description that is the result of the Myers Briggs Type
Indicator. If you have never done this, you need to. You will find it
enormously helpful in everything you do. Running with the trip metaphor
as it relates to rehearsals, consider the following:

E or I

The Extrovert thinks out loud with a group of people what possibilities
there are. He or she is energized by the group input and effort.
The Introvert researches in private. He or she comes out of the private,
quiet deliberation energized and convinced of the destination.

S or N

The Sensor focuses on the details necessary for the trip.
The iNtuitive focuses on the final destination.

T or F

The Thinker uses logic to make decisions as to where to go.
The Feeler looks at what is in the best interest of most of the people.

J or P

The Judger will have the entire trip planned.
The Perceiver hangs loose and goes with the flow.

For many years, I have begun my senior/graduate level Vocal and Choral
Pedagogy classes by a fairly in-depth study of the Myers Briggs Type
Indicators. I am not a psychologist, but even a cursory overview reveals
wonderful insights.

One of the most difficult things for nonprofessionals to do is to describe the
various personality types with complete equanimity. My own perspective
is from ENFJ and from teaching vocal students for 30 years who are mostly
ENFP. So, these are the types I know better. Let's look at some of our
personality traits that affect who we are as conductor and as tour guide!

The first choice is between Extrovert and Introvert. This is not about being
loud or being quiet. This is not about loving to be "on stage" or "in the
spotlight." We are actually on stage in rehearsals as well. This is about
how you charge your own batteries. Do you get energy from leading a
full car of folks or would you rather sit on a bus with just a book for
company? Are you more energized by a rehearsal room full of people, or
score preparation?

More than likely, you have chosen this career of conducting because you are energized by being around people. Your nonpreferred skills of spending time alone, studying your scores, making rehearsal plans, etc., must be learned and developed. In order to be successful, you must master the skills of an introvert, i.e., the quiet, alone preparation time required to do your job well. The opposite is also true. If you are an introvert who loves score study, you must learn the skills of the extrovert, although you will never actually become one. The Extrovert works through issues and processes out loud. The Introvert works through things much differently, mostly on his/her own and in quiet. The focus is on reflection.

Now you know you're going on a choral trip, and are now ready to decide on the destination and what music to sing. Being a person who is imaginative, creative, and full of possibilities, you decide where you are headed simply because you feel inspired to head to Timbuktu. Sure, there are others who would love for you to know all of the facts before you make such a decision. But you are certain because of a hunch. You are most likely categorized as Intuitive (N).

The Sensing people (S) would feel a lot better if you gathered and presented the facts that helped you come to your decision. In fact, they would really like for you to repeat a concert you did a couple of seasons ago because it is "tried and true."

You had a "feeling" you knew where you wanted to go and what you wanted to sing, but you were still torn by those who wanted all of the facts, the map, the description, the finances, etc. But you decided to select a destination because you knew it would be "life-changing." You may not have known all of the facts and it may not have been the "logical" choice, but you knew that everyone going on the trip would truly benefit. You used your heart more than your head. You are most likely a Feeler (F). Your opposite organized all the information in a logical, objective way and drew a conclusion. They used their head over their heart and came to a logical decision. They are the Thinkers (T).

You have chosen your destination, feel good about it, and have a plan that you know will work. Weeks before the departure date, you may even have an excel spreadsheet mapping the trip minute by minute. You are said to deal with the outer world in a judging manner (J). Your counterpart's preference is to "wing it." They want to take a trip where you can "hang loose." They are the ones who pass out music well into the rehearsal period because they can't make up their mind in advance. They are Perceivers (P). Judgers (J) are good multitaskers. They make lists in order to keep all of the balls they are juggling in the air. The Perceivers focus on one ball at a time, if any balls at all.

Stereotypical conductors are ENFJ: prone to Extraversion, Intuition, Feeling, and Judging.

Stereotypical singers are ENFP: prone to Extraversion, Intuition, Feeling, and Perceiving.

So, what are your letters? ___ ___ ___ ___

In *Introduction to Type in Organizations*, the authors describe people falling into these categories as follows:

ENFJs are: "warm, empathetic, responsive, and responsible, highly attuned to the emotions, needs and motivations of others; find potential in everyone, want to help others fulfill their potential; may act as catalysts for individual and group growth; loyal, responsive to praise and criticism; sociable, facilitate others in a group, provide inspiring leadership." ENFJs like their lives to be organized and will work to bring closure to ambiguous situations. ENFJs may be overly sensitive to criticism, real or imagined, and accept the judgments of others too readily. They sometimes overlook details required to realize their ideals. Under great stress, ENFJs may find themselves suddenly and uncharacteristically critical and fault-finding with others.

ENFPs are: "enthusiastic, insightful, innovative, versatile, and tireless in pursuit of new possibilities; enjoy working on teams to bring about change related to making things better for people." ENFPs may overlook relevant details and facts, may overextend and try to do too much, may procrastinate, may move on to new ideas or projects without completing those already started. They need to pay attention to and focus on key details, set priorities, learn to say "no," and apply time management skills to meet goals.

Does one of the above describe you? I encourage you to study this more thoroughly. The important thing for you to remember is that you will have people in your chorus of every single personality type. And if you have a board of directors, it will be made up of every single type, as are your principals, pastors or accompanists! One of the keys to getting along with all of them is to understand how differently they approach things!

The Circles of Our Lives

A wonderful friend and composer, David Brunner, has penned the text and music to a beautiful composition. If you have not heard or performed this stunning piece, run, don't walk, to your music provider. If all you do is sit at your piano and sing it to yourself, you will thank me for the recommendation.

Long before I ever came across this song, I had thought about how our lives can be defined in circles. Throughout the book, I will give you several examples of what I mean. Here is a portion of David's text.

Again, again we come and go, changing.
Hands join, unjoin in love and fear, grief and joy.
The circles turn, each giving into each, into all.
Only music keeps us here,
Only music keeps us here.

Each by all the others held.
In the hold of hands and eyes we turn in pairs
That joining, joining each to all again.

And then we turn aside, alone,
Out of the sunlight gone
Into the darker circles of return.

Within the circles of our lives
We dance the circles of the years.
The circle of the seasons within the circles of the years;
The cycles of the moon within the circles of the seasons;
The circles of our reasons
Within the cycles of the moon.

Again, again we come and go changed, changing.
Hands join, unjoin in love and fear, grief and joy.
The circles turn, each giving into each, into all.
Only music keeps us here,
Only music keeps us here.

Circle #1: Who are you?

Giver
Leader
Counselor
Friend
Parent
Sibling

Circle #2:   What is the career you have chosen?

Conductor
Teacher
Administrator

Minister of
Music

How do they intersect?

Example #1: Healthy cross section.

Giver - Teacher
Leader - Conductor
Counselor - Minister
Parent - Sibling
Friend

Example #2: Not so healthy.

Giver Parent Sibling Friend

Teacher
Conductor
Administrator
Minister

There is so much more to life than just "what you do" for a living. You
are not defined by "what you do," but by "who you are."

Chapter 3

Selecting the Destination
Museum or amusement park?

KNOW THYSELF
KNOW THY SINGERS
KNOW THY AUDIENCE

To thine own self, singers, and audience be true.
Be true in that order, or it won't work.

There was a day when, if you were planning a trip, you simply visited or called a travel agent. There was no other way. Hard to imagine. Today, it is all available on the internet. ALL of it. The travel agent industry, as we knew it, has been completely shut down.

Several years ago, the only place to learn anything about concerts or repertoire was from our teachers, at conventions, or from other concerts that we might attend. Sometimes our only choices for repertoire came from whatever we found in the library of the chorus we were conducting... before PDFs and copy machines.

Going to concerts and conventions is like gathering travel brochures.

We sit down with our families, friends, partners and dream about trips and vacations! Where can we go? When can we go? How often can we go?

Decisions, decisions:

How many trips can we take? How many concerts will we do?

How many trips are obligatory? – to Grandma's perhaps, or the "cash cow" (oops, I'm sorry, did I say "cash cow"?). I meant wonderful, meaningful holiday concert(s).

How many trips are just for fun and can be exotic?
(We just don't do enough of these.)

Your chorus needs to know why you have selected certain destinations. They need to know why you selected the museum instead of the amusement park. Why did you take them on an educational field trip instead of the swimming pool? They need to see the balance you are trying to achieve in their overall experience.

Most choruses have multiple personalities and multiple purposes. Those can include, but are not limited to:

- Entertain
- Educate
- Unite
- Uplift

At that point, it is a question of motivation:

- A well-articulated mission/vision statement for the group.
- A feeling of belonging and that giving so much time and money to a hobby is worthwhile.
- Interesting, innovative, fun, and challenging programming.

And it all boils down to balance. If you only go to museums, you are going to attract and keep a certain kind of student. If you only go to the amusement park, you attract another type. We want to have all types in our choruses so that we are well-rounded in what we do and in who eventually comes to hear us sing. This variety carries over to rehearsal.

Our audience has grown to expect the unexpected. Early in my career with the Turtle Creek Chorale, as concerts began to get more interesting and colorful, audience members would say, "This was the best yet. How are you going to top yourself next time?" I would thank them and answer "I am not, but the next concert will be so different, you won't even try to compare them." This was the key and has certainly served our chorus very well in providing a variety of musical experiences. Certainly there are choruses that find a niche and are very successful staying in a more narrow genre and developing a loyal following. It simply has not been my experience.

Planning a concert and an entire season of four or five major concerts becomes a puzzle trying to hit on all cylinders. There is such incredible variety in the music from which we get to choose, only the lazy need present boring choral concerts.

Expect the Extraordinary

When you approach the music you are making with your chorus, expect the extraordinary. If you don't, you will never achieve it. Assume you are going to make exquisite music and nothing less. This means coloring outside the lines. Simply following instructions and doing exactly what the music dictates is not enough. Read the great reviews of incredible performances. Rarely do they say, "The conductor succeeded brilliantly in doing exactly what was on the printed page." More often, they say, "The conductor made the music his/her own, bringing creativity and life to the score." Don't forget, this takes time. And you must also know your audience and what they like and will tolerate!

THE PARABLE OF MISGUIDED TOUR GUIDE
Choosing the wrong destination

Choosing the wrong destination is a malady suffered by many of the choruses we hear year in and year out. This is exactly what happened to DaWayne. He simply chose a destination that didn't fit those traveling or those waiting at the other end (the audience). It was like taking 2-year-olds to see the great museums of Europe, or senior citizens for a weekend at Hurricane Harbor water theme park. Here is his story. Any resemblance to real people and their stories is purely intentional. The names and faces have been changed to protect the guilty.

DaWayne was in his first year as the entire "music department" of a small, rural community college in the town where he grew up. He had two years of college on a B.A. degree before moving home. He was the obvious choice when the position became available. He taught all the music courses, directed the "pep" band for the girls' basketball games (they didn't have a boys' team), conducted the choir, and was the 4-H sponsor. His reward for working so hard was directing the combined choir and band concert at the end of the year featuring a "major work."

When he was at the state university, the choir in which he had sung performed Bach's B Minor Mass. He fell in love with it. Furthermore, he had read somewhere that playing Bach over a loudspeaker in the barn actually calmed the cows. They, in turn, gave sweeter milk. So this particular music combined both of his passions: Baroque and bovines. In fact, his plan was that one day he would do his Master's thesis on the Mass and its bucolic effect on farm animals. (I digress.)

He was convinced he had chosen well for the spring combined concert. He remembered it as being a pretty "long song," but also knew they could just take some cuts here and there if the folks got restless. He had worked so hard on it in college, he knew he could pull it off.

When the spring semester rolled around, enrollment in choir had dropped significantly due to the proverbial grapevine regarding the upcoming concert and softball season. Being a hometown boy, he was able to recruit quite well from the greater community. He got four basses who could sing the melody down an octave. He got a gaggle of sopranos who sounded like they were singing melismas while holding one note! He got two strong altos who ran the local beauty parlor, "Curl up and Dye." They could really reach the low notes due to chain-smoking and inhaled hair chemicals over the years. Two other altos were recruited to sing tenor. He was set!

The skirmish began at the first rehearsal when they realized they were to sing in a foreign language! But in the end, everyone jumped in and gave their best for DeWayne. Good news: there were some Catholics in the next town to help with the Latin.

They were just not ready for Bach, so it didn't work out so well. At the last minute, they were able to switch to an audience-favorite "cantata" the previous director had put together which included: "Dixie," "The Battle Hymn of the Republic," and "God Bless the USA." The day was saved.

What Was Wrong and What Can We Learn?

Think of being on a plane and the flight attendant makes the following announcement: "Welcome aboard Flight 333 headed for New York. If this is not your destination, please deplane immediately." We all chuckle, but no one ever gets off. If they have gotten that far, they are just too embarrassed to admit their mistake. They must figure that once they get to New York, they can connect to wherever it was they intended to go in the first place.

Whatever you sang and loved in college may not be appropriate for your own choir. There are many reasons for selecting particular repertoire: because you love it; because you think it will "be good" for them; because it stretches and challenges them. But if you select for those reasons, you may find out it wasn't the best idea after all. This has happened to all of us.

My Own Misguided Tour

One day, while driving, I began listening to a new CD I had purchased. Upon hearing Eric Whitacre's "When David Heard," performed by the BYU choir, I literally had to pull over because I was weeping almost uncontrollably. I played the recording for my mixed chorus and they had the same reaction. So I ordered it. The chorus consisted of adults – and not young adults – that rehearsed once a week. We launched into it. In no time, I knew it was going to thoroughly defeat us. The basic vocal requirements were beyond the capabilities of my singers, but they loved the piece. Time to punt. We were all disappointed, but also relieved not to have to sit in rehearsal trying to get those "mature" sopranos to float straight tones in the very top of their ranges. We had, however, managed to gather all the stray dogs in the area by the end of rehearsal. Some were pretty good sopranos!

At the end of that concert session, when we had not performed several of the pieces I had selected, we were discussing the season in an open forum (another questionable decision on my part). One of the more honest, outspoken sopranos said, "Would you please select music that is more in line with our capabilities? We want to please you. We want to be the best we can be. However, this year hasn't been so much fun because you have had to be on our backs all year!" Boy, did I learn an important lesson.

THE OPPOSITE IS JUST AS BAD. There are many conductors who have excellent singers and kill their choirs by selecting music far beneath their capabilities. Either way, it won't work. One of the most difficult and important tasks the conductor has is to select the most appropriate music for his/her ensembles.

Don't Pander to, Underestimate, or Insult Your Singers or Your Audience. You Will Pay a Huge Price.

CIRCLES

What are the things we have to take into consideration when choosing a destination? Which are the most important to you? To your choir? To your audience? To your board? To your principal? To your pastor?

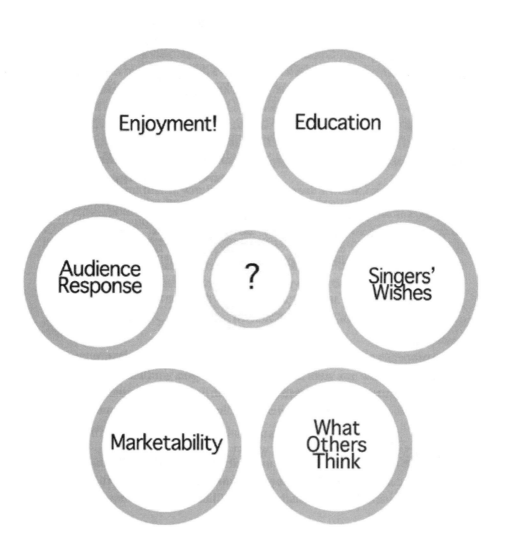

Chapter 4

Who Will Help You Along the Way?
If you are the driver, who is the nagivator (sic)?

Back-seat driving. Don't you just love it? It's why a friend of mine (thanks, Louis) coined the word "Nagivator" instead of Navigator. (Most often, instructions offered from the proverbial "back seat" include a fair amount of judgment!) "I said turn left." "I told you we were almost there." "I distinctly remember asking you to slow down when you got to the third tree." "I would have taken a different tempo." "I would have used a little wider dynamic palette." Back-seat driving in rehearsal is the perfect job for those passive/aggressive people in your choir.

Some years ago, we had such a singer. We sang one of our pieces for the upcoming concert–beautifully, I thought. At the end of rehearsal, this member raised his hand and asked in a rather sarcastic tone, "Is that concert tempo?" The entire chorus just held its breath. The question may have been an innocent one, but one asked with the completely wrong tone of voice. The singer's dislike of the chosen tempo was quite apparent and he felt the need to point that out to everyone.

What was my answer to his question? "I guess you'll know the tempo at the concert when I find out myself." Another half-joking reply might be, "the tempo will depend on what I had for dinner before the concert or what kind of mood I am in." There is more truth to that than I dare admit. But it also depends on so many other factors:

- The acoustics of the performance space (If the room is dead, the tempos are quicker and vice versa.)
- The temperature in the room
- How the chorus is singing
- The reaction of the audience (If I sense they are nodding off, you can bet the tempos are going to perk up a bit.)
- My own A.D.D.

While we might like to pretend that a metronome marking is something that carries a weight of Biblical proportion in our conducting, that would be burying our heads in the sand concerning the above. This takes us back to the wise person who suggested that the music on the page is merely a suggestion.

How many of your singers are backseat-drivers? Don't answer that, I already know–and most of them are sitting in the back seats! When your adult chorus membership includes choir directors, it gets worse. We do make some of the worst choir members on earth!

Of course, there are those who would like to be in your place on the podium because they are convinced they could do better. But there are also the innocents. You know the ones. They are the brand-new members who open their mouths and insert their feet until they realize their mouths are meant for singing while in choral rehearsals!

OK, I've made fun of the Nagivator because we all know and love them. But we also need them. A true <u>Navigator</u> is going to read the map with no input. This doesn't really help. The Nagivator, while perhaps mildly annoying, cares enough to throw in the extra advice along the way, even if you don't always want to hear it.

Of course, you can't make this journey alone. Though we would like to think we are completely self-sufficient, we aren't. The more help you are willing to ask for, the better the trip and the destination are going to be. This is exactly why I decided to ask my colleagues for their input. You will read their thoughts a little later and they are fantastic.

You Can Never Have Too Many Tools!

Some of the tools I am going to list are invaluable. Just be careful how you use them and how you refer to them. I recently sat on a panel interviewing a choral director for a fairly prestigious position. His resumé was impressive. He wrote that he had studied with my friend James Jordan, as well as other luminaries. Now that was impressive. James is a brilliant teacher/conductor, so I asked the candidate where he had studied with James. He looked as if I had just told him he had forgotten to wear pants to the interview. He hadn't actually studied "with" him, but he had watched one of his videos! Ouch. Watching videos, or now DVDs, is a good thing, but it does not really qualify as "studying" with that person.

What resources do you have on your shelf, or among colleagues or even chorus members?

When I first arrived at my job with the Turtle Creek Chorale 19 years ago, one of the members asked a simple (to him) question: "When do you want the Music Advisory Committee to meet?" Well, I had never heard of such a thing and being young and brash (now I am just old and brash), I said something like, "How about the 12th? Of never." In hindsight, there were so many other kinder and gentler ways I could have conveyed my message. Hindsight. Oh, well. That committee was indeed disbanded because I couldn't imagine what purpose it could serve.

Now, all these years later, I have somewhat reinstated that concept. In some ways having 25 music teachers or music professionals in my chorus has been lucky. Throughout the year, I gather all the music and sort it into big piles. During the early part of the summer, they are invited to come sing the things that have been set aside in the "possible" pile. Obviously, I don't put things in that pile that I do not like or do not want to conduct. We divide the day into concerts for the year and have a great time discussing repertoire and other people in the chorus. We have lunch brought in and "share" our thoughts about music, the chorus, and the concert season, etc.

This has some wonderful advantages. There are definitely times when they have absolutely loved a piece that was near the bottom of my "possible" pile and it has become a chorus favorite. The reverse has happened as well. I will go in thinking this is just the cat's "meow" (having played through it with my formidable keyboard prowess), and they just hate it. Most often, their recommendation is followed. There are also pieces that are introduced with, "We will not be voting on this one, just enjoy singing it because it is nonnegotiable." This exercise truly does give them a sense of ownership in the repertoire for the season and also gives me someone to blame if things go terribly wrong. There are a few who do not like anything, of course, but I know that going into the exercise. Often, when they really, really don't like something, experience has proved it's probably a winner.

There is a list of some resources on page 134.

28

Sharing the "Nagivator" responsibilities

This may seem like overkill to you, but it works–no matter the size of your chorus. Our chorus is divided into four sections, each with two types of "leaders." Each section has Musical Section Leaders and Administrative Section Leaders. The number of MSLs and ASLs is obviously relative to the size of your own chorus.

The Musical Section Leaders are the ones who are in charge of making sure the section has the music and the artistic information they need. They are the ones who receive the Musical Mishap forms which are discussed later. They move around within the section and listen for problems I might not hear. Four musical section leaders are in each of the four sections, which is what it takes for 250 singers in a chorus. One coordinator and one accompanist are among the four.

The Administrative Section Leaders take the roll for each section and generally manage the nonmusical issues that arise. The roll is taken again after break to catch those who couldn't possibly stay for both halfs of rehearsal! Other administrative responsibilities such as taking up money, wardrobe issues, etc. are also taken care of by ASLs.

The MSLs and ASLs are simply liaisons between the conductor and members, helping distribute the responsibility throughout the chorus. The number of questions and the number of announcements made during rehearsals is also minimized.

Some people should simply not be allowed to help "nagivate" your journey.

They are:

1. Someone with his/her own agenda that does not mesh with the organization.
2. Someone who does not have your best interest in mind.
3. Your best friend, spouse or family member.
4. Someone unqualified to express opinions.
5. Someone who wants your job.

Chapter 5

Mapping Out the Trip/Rehearsals
Triple R – Rehearsal, Rehabilitation, and Rescue

Calling on "Triple A" can really help in planning a trip. The American Automobile Association will actually help you map out the trip in every way. They will let you know if there is construction along the way; how far apart the gas stations are; the location of rest stops; and the sights along the way that you shouldn't miss – and a few you should. They will also come to your aid if you have a flat tire or car trouble. So, who is going to do that on our rehearsal journey toward our concert?

This book is your Triple R!

Rehearsal Technique

What is rehearsal technique? Do I have one? Where can I get one? The answer is, you do have one (whether you know it or not). When asked, you might say, "I don't have an actual 'rehearsal technique' per se." Oh, yes you do. Whatever routine you do with your chorus on a regular basis *is* your rehearsal technique, whether or not you have ever thought of it in those terms.

Technique is the ability to consistently repeat the same patterns of coordination.

Whatever it is you are doing day after day, week after week, is YOUR TECHNIQUE! For better or for worse, in sickness and in health. Given this, then, some reasonable questions are things such as:

- How do you start each rehearsal?
- How do you end each rehearsal?
- Do you keep the energy up throughout?
- Are you really listening to how they are singing?
- Are they singing as well when they leave as when they arrived?
- Do you have help planning rehearsals?

Let's assume that the destination is now clear. How do we get there? What are the resources at our hands to help us with this?

It is time to log onto CHORALQUEST.COM
Wouldn't it be great if there really were such a thing? It would be the Mapquest of the choral experience.

1. Enter the beginning point in the journey (first rehearsal).
2. Enter the destination (concert).
3. Voila! Your rehearsals are all planned!

Even though there is no CHORALQUEST.COM, information at your finger tips has grown amazingly and the resources are mind-boggling. Look at the list of Web sites on page 136. Each of those will have numerous links to even more resources for you to peruse.

But there are some obvious things we need to look at before we can really plan well. Here are some of the things to think about:

Where are rehearsals?
How long are rehearsals?
How many rehearsals are there?
What are the conditions like in the rehearsal hall?
Is there anything you can do to make them better?
Can you be heard?
Can you be seen?
Do you have a good accompanist?
Do you have a good sound system?
How are the chairs?
How are the risers?

Spice it up

In *The Perfect Blend*, all of the analogies regarding warm-ups were about food. That works for rehearsals as well. We all eat and some of us even cook. Regardless of how little, we all know how to pick up a recipe and make something, even if it is out of a box or in the microwave. We would never think of just going to the cabinet and start throwing things together with no rhyme or reason. What if you just threw in all dry ingredients or all wet, mushy, soggy ones? What if all of the ingredients were things you couldn't even pronounce, like some of our concerts?

Every time you put together a rehearsal, you are creating a new recipe. Granted, the main course may remain much the same. But you have to use a variety of spices every once in awhile or your "family" is going to throw it back in your face (or they should). If you feed them exactly the same rehearsal meal day after day or week after week, they go home unsatisfied, and worse, they tell everyone they know not to come to your house to eat because they'll be getting the same thing every single time. Imagine wanting to go to a restaurant that advertises "we cook the same thing every single day, with no seasoning, no creativity, and no variety. Do not come to our restaurant if you are looking for a taste sensation."

Creative rehearsals—what's the point?

In public school and university choral programs, we may think there is little compelling reason to worry about flow or pacing or motivating the singers in rehearsal. We may think there is no need to be concerned about the enjoyment factor or taking responsibility for wasting students' time. Nice if it happens, but if not, it is not what we are there to teach, or so we think. Yet we are training singers who will one day have their own choirs. And at the end of the year, they do have a choice. They can switch to band, orchestra, drama, sports or auto mechanics.

Say "No" to "Time-shares"

There is something appealing about buying into a time-share for your vacationing. On the other hand, there is a huge drawback. It is the same destination, and therefore, the very same trip each time. While this may be an inexpensive route, and certainly takes no creativity on your part, there is also no adventure. It is the same old, same old.

Is this what your rehearsals and concerts are like? Are your singers simply buying into the same old, same old? Chances are they won't buy into it for very long. Perhaps you have already made the leap to adventurous programming, but just haven't figured out how to transfer that variety and spice to your rehearsals.

Rumor has it that one of the legends of choral music used to begin his rehearsals the same way every week, for years and years. The first 15 minutes of rehearsal were the same warm-ups and had little to do with what was to follow. Apparently, the members caught on fairly quickly and began arriving 15 minutes late every week just to avoid the tedium.

Breathe! Let Go of Those Little Demons Saying: "What would my college professor think?"

It doesn't matter what your professor would think. He or she does not have to suffer through your boring, predictable rehearsals! Even if you have bought into the time-share that will remain in the family for eternity, there are ways to spice up even that scenario.

The same is true of your rehearsals. Start with simple things. Break up the time creatively. Look at all of the possibilities. Observe other peoples' rehearsals. All too often we do not **study** what our colleagues do in rehearsal. We watch their performances and just imagine what their rehearsals might be like. I am certain other conductors would be thrilled to allow us into their rehearsals to learn from them–the good, the bad, and the ugly. If you came up with one new idea to help your own rehearsals be better, it would be worth the time spent.

If you think boring rehearsals are an issue in your work, you are probably asking yourself, "How can I begin to change what I have been doing for years?" Here is the answer: Make a list of the many possibilities. Keep it on hand for when you are down in the dumps and think you can't face another rehearsal without screaming or hurting someone.

25 IDEAS TO PERK UP REHEARSAL

1. Do five fun warm-ups!
2. Sing a portion of one of the songs.
3. Talk about the text of one of the upcoming pieces you
   have chosen.
4. Have someone read it!
5. Sing a little bit.
6. Do some sight-reading just for fun.
7. Talk about the composer and the librettist.
8. Do some fun vocalises that make the singers move.
9. Ask one of the singers to describe what a song means
   to him or her.
10. Sing some more.
11. Make your announcements.
12. Divide into two choirs and sing for each other.
13. Do some more warm-ups.
14. Listen to another chorus sing on a CD.
15. Read portions of one of Dr. Seelig's books to the
    class.
16. Sing some more.
17. Do a memory pop test on what you have just sung.
18. Ask the singers for their best memory of singing.
19. Take roll.
20. Do some choreography.
21. Talk about the last concert, or the next one.
22. Rehearse one difficult passage you want them to
    remember.
23. Ask if there are any other announcements.
24. Sing their favorite song!
25. Tell them how much you appreciate them!

Assigned Seating

This is something that works very well for school or professional choirs. They don't really have a choice. Sometimes those of us who work in community or church choirs think it will work there as well. It has been my experience that it does not. Part of the reason our singers volunteer so much time is for a social outlet. They may join to be with friends or because of friends, or to make new ones. While assigned seating may sound like a good idea on paper, they may not really like the people assigned to sit by them. They won't keep coming back week after week. It is important that they enjoy the one, two or three hours they are going to spend in your chorus. I recommend placing only the singers who might be potential tonal problems. Again, it is your job to find the balance between the social and "business" sides of your chorus.

Aural Modeling

What is in your mind's ear? Do you have a favorite choral recording? Do you even listen to choral music? You don't have to answer that out loud. Whatever you listen to consistently helps set your tonal preferences for your own chorus. You know it when you hear it, you just may not know how to get there. Your chorus will only sing as beautifully as you can imagine them singing. And only as beautifully as you are able to translate that imagined tone to them via the choral technique you are teaching them. But first comes that aural ideal of yours. There are choral techniques you obviously admire and some you avoid (or should).

Do you play your favorite choral groups for your singers? Can you describe for them why you like the sound (and how you hope to achieve it with them)?

If they have not heard anyone "better" than themselves, they are striving toward a goal housed only in <u>your</u> head.

Top 5

Choose your Top 5 recordings. They can be single pieces or excerpts from a larger work. Burn a CD with portions of your Top 5 in one place where you can listen to them consecutively. What is it that draws you to each of them? Is there a common thread? Does that tell you something about what you are striving for in your own work with your own choruses? You might want to play this for your chorus.

Bottom 5

Now, for fun, compile a CD with your least favorite five choral moments. Don't put the names of the performing groups on it, just in case someone finds it!

Communication – More is better

As mentioned earlier, too much information and research into the music you are asking them to sing can lead your chorus to overload. There can never be too much information, however, regarding communicating the countless details it takes to mount a choral program. No doubt you already pass out information on a weekly basis to your members about rehearsals, performances, additional meetings, fund raisers, etc.

Two possibilities: phone and e-mail.

These days, electronic phone trees are not expensive to purchase. You can have every single member on a phone system that will phone them with updated messages. You can divide them into groups on the same tool so you can phone one section, the officers, or any group you choose.

More important and much more current are e-mail groups. Every Tuesday night, we pass out a hard copy of important information in "Tim's Notes." The following day, we e-mail those notes (sometimes updated from the night before) to every member. This way, no one can ever say they didn't know about the schedule or changes or what to wear! If they don't know, they didn't read their notes, hard copy or e-mailed copy. For a time, we had a few members without e-mail, so we mailed notes to them. We are now at 100 percent of the membership with e-mail capability. All calendars and information are also posted on the chorus Website. Communication saves my life when singers say, "You didn't tell us there was rehearsal or what to wear or when to show up." I just say, "Check your e-mail!"

Announcements in rehearsal – Head 'em up, move 'em out.

There was a time when there would be a line of people who wanted to make announcements at rehearsal. Some had relevant things to say. Some just wanted to hear themselves talk and most often about events that were three months away and had nothing to do with the chorus. This has been remedied by one person doing all announcements.

If a person has not gotten their announcement to the appropriate person in time to be included in the printed notes, they hand a written announcement to the officer in charge of announcements that particular night. The officer can then make a judgment if the announcement is urgent or timely. If not, it can go in the following week's printed notes! This has hugely curtailed lengthy and meaningless announcements.

Attendance

This is always the issue in a volunteer chorus, especially when each member pays dues in order to sing. It is difficult to say "If you don't come to every rehearsal, I'm going to make you stop paying dues." Something is lost in the translation. We have tried everything and finally have come up with the best system I have ever encountered.

The point, after all, is to make it possible for the members to all sing, but also not punish those who come to every rehearsal by allowing someone to miss too many rehearsals and then perform poorly.

At the beginning of each concert period, the Administrative Section Leaders and the conductor determine the actual number of rehearsals for that particular concert. Let's say there are 15. At that point, they decide what the threshold is for missing rehearsals. An average might be three.

Everyone is treated the same. When a person has missed the assigned number of rehearsals, they are then notified that they will be required to sing a Concert Preparedness Audition two weeks before the performance. At that point, the conductor and whatever committee of "judges" he/she chooses will listen to the group assembled to determine if they know the music well enough to perform. The audition is not difficult, but simply a hurdle that everyone knows they must clear if they are to perform.

With this system, the singers know exactly what is expected. They also know if something comes up and they miss more than three rehearsals, they are not automatically out of the performance if they do the required work. The singers who made all of the rehearsals know that you have required something extra of those who missed, so they feel good. The singers who miss more than three, and don't know their music, usually bow out of that concert rather than embarrass themselves at an audition.

Chapter 6

Packing for the Trip – Physically and Emotionally
We all have baggage, but will it fit in the trunk?

Did you ever get in the car with your family or friends and just start driving? I did. Once! I must admit it was really fun. We actually just got in the car and decided to pick a direction and just drive. It is also something that we wouldn't do very often, regardless of where we lived. It's hard to know what to pack!

What are you going to pack for the trip?
What kind of "packer" are you when you take a trip?
Too much, too little, or just the right amount?

I wonder if there is a correlation in how you pack for a trip and how you prepare for rehearsals? Some things you can pick up along the way (or even fake) but not all of it. This is not one of those "6 months across Europe with just a backpack" trips. You'll definitely need more than that. But do you need the entire set of Louis Vuitton luggage? Probably not. Sometimes the music changes from what's planned – there is a road you want to take that was not in your plan

Pack too much? Do you always bring home clean, unused clothes from your trips? You probably do the same in rehearsals. Do you always plan way more than you ever accomplish?

Pack too little? Do you have to recycle used underclothes on your last three days? If you are not prepared, they'll catch you every time! "If I forget something, I can always buy it when I get there." This is under-planning. You have to "wing it" for every rehearsal – wasting everyone's time. It won't work to just say "Sing it again" as you wash out your underwear one more time in the motel sink.

Pack for your rehearsal as if your life depended on it – the life of your choir certainly does.

Packing list for rehearsal (for you and the passengers):

1. Music
2. Dictionaries (foreign language and musical)
3. Writing utensil
4. Colored pencils/highlighters
5. Metronome
6. Rehearsal plan
7. Clean handkerchiefs (for sweat and tears)
8. Sample CDs
9. Sample DVDs
10. Refreshments (at least water)
11. Hand-held recorders
12. MP3 files on a Website
13. Choreography on a Website
14. Tylenol or Dramamine
15. Thick skin
16. Phone number for a good therapist
17. An adult beverage waiting at home

Don't forget the maps!

You need a plan. But everyone doesn't need to know what it is! You don't pass out maps to everyone in the car!

Different kinds of maps for the journey

There are different kinds of maps you will need for any trip. Certainly, you need the overall map of how to get there, but you will also need a map of the city you are visiting. A map of the neighborhood where you will spend most of your time will be helpful as well.

The same is true of the choral journey. We have already discussed the big-picture map, which is the concerts you are planning for the entire season or year. This is your **Season Map**. In addition to that, there is the concert map. Those of us who put together choral concerts with 15-18 separate pieces must learn this art better than almost anything we do. There is magic in how you pace your program. This is your **Concert Map**.

There is the **Rehearsal Map** as well. In order not to have the "cookie-cutter" rehearsals previously described, you can look at the entire rehearsal period as a whole. If you have 10 weeks of rehearsals before reaching your destination, how can you make them interesting and different from each other. This can be done with the following: changing the order in which you rehearse; dividing the chorus and having them sing for each other; rehearsing in chairs one week, on risers or in a circle another; playing CDs or showing DVDs of other choruses performing. There are a variety of ways to mix it up and keep them guessing and coming back.

And there is the individual **Song Map**. A vocal landscape map is a great tool in your own preparation. Such a landscape tracks the contour of the piece, the loudest and softest measures, difficult sections, text setting, etc. Included can be vowels or leaps or chords that may be challenging. The landscape will assist you in the creation of vocalises for each of those places. One may be found in *The Perfect Blend*.

Packing for the trip – emotionally. We all have baggage, but does it match?

The trick is all in your outlook. Two teachers arrive at the beginning of the school year and hear their choir for the first time.

One says, "It's horrible. They simply can't sing. I'll never get anything out of them. I deserve better."

Another says, "It's wonderful. They can't sing. There's nowhere to go but up. God bless 'em, I can't lose!"

Rehearsal is the most important activity you do! Period.

Rehearsal is a time when your singers have entrusted you with their most precious gift – their time – to do with as you wish. It is a serious responsibility. It is not your time to whine, complain, or let whatever is happening in your own life affect your performance in rehearsal. The singers don't need to know if you are tired or sick or just sick and tired. It is not their problem. Your job is to take them out of whatever they are currently experiencing in their own lives and use the music to lift everyone to a higher place. That can't happen if you begin with any disclaimer.

This has nothing to do with being vulnerable with your singer family. Of course, you need to be vulnerable to a point and let them share in your life's ups and downs. But not at the beginning of a rehearsal and maybe not in rehearsal at all.

If you were to ask my singers how I feel about rehearsals, they would say pretty much the same thing: he is prepared; he is prepared to have fun; he is driven to complete the tasks that he has set forth for the rehearsal; he is "on." Most of the time.

There is a fine line between being friendly, open, vulnerable and TMI (Too Much Information!). I once mentored a young conductor of a community chorus. In addition to the chorus, she was beginning a new junior high choral job during the day – somewhat akin to herding water buffalo and hyenas and making them sing together. When she arrived at 7:00 p.m. each Monday night, things went from bad to worse. Normally the first words out of her mouth were something like, "I'm sorry if I am rather bitchy or out of sorts tonight. I had a really rough day at school. I'll try not to take it out on you." Ouch!

The members in this community chorus also worked all day. They grabbed food for their kids, got them settled, grabbed their music folders, checked to see if they had a pencil and everything they would need for rehearsal. As they rushed out the door, they grabbed the money they collected from selling lovely little crocheted hairspray can covers to raise money for the next choir trip and the 10 tickets they had not been able to sell to the next fund raiser, a concert at Chucky Cheese. In the car on the way to rehearsal, they began to put all of that hysteria behind them.

Mile by mile, the cares of the day slipped away. The stress at work was slipping away. The worries were replaced with lofty thoughts: Choir is my favorite time of the entire week. Singing is the joy of my life. I get to see friends who I only see once a week. I get to forget what I do by day and become something different. Something better. I arrive. I wave at my friends, slip in a little happy gossip, and find my place. I haven't felt this good in days, knowing the glorious experience of becoming a small part of something greater – a choir, not a bunch of solo singers.

And then from the podium I hear, "I've had a really bad day. The kids at school blah blah blah and my headache won't go away and blah blah blah. And I think, "she is getting paid to stand up there. Actually, I am the one paying for the privilege of sitting here listening to this. Not for long!"

DON'T DO IT. DON'T DO IT. Prepare yourself for every rehearsal. Yes, prepare musically. But more than that, prepare yourself mentally, emotionally, and spiritually.

This is absolutely the wrong time and place for TMI – either about the music you are singing or, most especially, about you and how you are feeling and how things are going with you in your life. Trust me. At that very moment, they do not care. If you wonder about member recruitment and retention, check what kind of atmosphere you are creating at rehearsals.

The only way to remain consistent, on task, focused, and avoid winging it by simply telling stories about yourself, is to have a rehearsal plan. And stick to it!

Love the Process More Than the Product
The means is more important than the end.

When you take your family or friends on a trip, you want them to have a wonderful time – both in getting there and while they are there. We take care to make the trip fun and enjoyable. Certainly we want to leave all the cares of home behind to explore new and exciting things. Otherwise, we would just stay at home!

When your singers join you on a trip, you want the same thing. You want them to enjoy the trip and the destination. At that first rehearsal (when they get into the car), you want them to:

- Leave their worries and troubles at the door (they may decide not to pick them back up at the door when they leave).
- Get their blood flowing and bodies ready to sing.
- Breathe.
- Relax.
- Concentrate on their instrument, not notes or rhythms or text.
- Hear the sounds you are wanting apart from the music.
- Work toward unification of vowels and concentrate on intonation.
- Connect with each other and with you.
- Experience something exciting and amazing they could never do on their own – becoming a choir.

This is your time to focus on them, not your chance to have them focus on you and your issues!

You have a captive audience. They either have to be there or have chosen to be there. For the most part, they aren't going to jump out of a moving car once you get started. But just because they are stuck, you still need to treat them with the utmost respect for their gift of time and energy.

TAKE NOTE!

You have to "gear" yourself up for the ride.

You have to be excited about the ups and downs.

Whatever it takes to "pump you up" is what you have to do.

Hint:
If you have a secret calendar starting with the
first day of the year and you mark off each day
one by one, you are probably not savoring the journey.

Chapter 7

Timing is Everything
How long will it take to get there?

There are two ways to go about this — and it's all about math.

Select a destination.
Determine how long it will take to get there.
Plan your trip based on that.

or

Determine how long you have for your trip.
Decide how far you can get in that amount of time.
Plan your destination accordingly.

In the same vein:

Look at the concert repertoire you want to do.
Determine how many rehearsals it will take to achieve your goal.
You have your plan.

or

Determine how many rehearsals you have.
Decide what kind of repertoire you can achieve in that time.
There is your concert!

Have you ever considered a formula for how much rehearsal it should take your singers to get prepared? Bear with me. I was considering math as a major, remember?

A two-hour concert has 90 minutes of actual music.

This is the calculation where many of us go astray. We somehow think a concert that lasts for two hours contains two hours of music. But that is really a 2 1/2 hour concert once all is said and done (at least!). In our calculations, we forget to factor in a 20-minute intermission, massive applause, and some well-placed and appropriate comments by the conductor, principal, preacher, chairperson of the board, executive director, etc.

I repeat, a two-hour concert has two halfs, each containing 45 minutes of music. At an average of 5 minutes per song, this is a total of 18 songs in a two-hour concert.

If you are using music in your concert, one five-minute song will take one hour of rehearsal to learn well. Therefore, the minimum rehearsal you would need for 18 songs is 18 hours of rehearsal. This is actual rehearsal time, not taking into account all of the other things that you have to do such as taking attendance, announcements, sight-reading exercises, warming up, interruptions, etc. Factoring those in, you might need 25 hours of rehearsal time for a two-hour concert using music.

If you are memorizing the concert – and hopefully that is a given – you are going to need more time. One five-minute song will take two hours of rehearsal to learn it well and memorize. Therefore, your 18 songs will require 36 hours of actual rehearsal. Add in the extraneous stuff and you are up to about 45 hours of rehearsal.

This works out to an average of 4.5 hours of rehearsal per week in a concert period of 10 weeks in order to memorize a 2-hour concert or 90 minutes of music. There are times when our chorus has a 6-week turnaround between memorized concerts. This obviously just means more rehearsal time each week.

These numbers are estimates. Each chorus learns differently, but it should give you a good idea of a starting point. If you don't plan well, you can always add rehearsals at the end just before reaching the destination. Not a good idea. More on that later.

There are other considerations in planning rehearsals for a given concert. Finances are always a consideration in how long you have to pull off a concert. These can include rehearsal hall rental, accompanist pay, perhaps security for the parking lot or even utilities. Then you begin to add in the cost of dress rehearsal in the concert hall (and tech rehearsal in the hall, if you are lucky). In addition, you have instrumentalists' costs to figure in as well.

It still comes down to math!

Chapter 8

Recruitment and Motivation for Those Traveling
"Do we get to see the world's largest ball of string?"

The potential pool of fellow travelers is huge!

According to the NEA 1997 Survey of Public Participation in the Arts, one in ten Americans sings in some kind of organized group. This means 20.3 million people are singing in groups! This is far more people than jog on a regular basis. Will we ever run out of singers? Not likely. We will run out of runners first.

So, who will travel with you? Who will join your community chorus and why? Who will sign up for your choir at school or become a loyal church choir member?

There is some fascinating new research about why people choose to do certain things and what actually motivates them. You have read in *The Perfect Blend* about the famous "g" words that we use as motivation. In church, we use "guilt." In school, we use the "grade." In community choruses, we use the "goal." It is up to you, the visionary, to define the goal. For most choruses and most singers, a perfect performance of the music is not enough. Not these days.

Motivation

We recently went through a period when the morale of the Turtle Creek Chorale just seemed to drop. It wasn't serious, but a malaise just settled over the chorus and it seemed I couldn't get them out of it. Guilt was the starter: they had signed up (agreed) to sing a particular concert and it didn't matter if they didn't like it, they needed to honor their word. Then came the people in the audience to whom they owed something. Finally, I told them how good they were going to feel when they mastered this difficult music.

One of my members (thanks, Todd) introduced me to some new research and an article by Kennon L. Callahan entitled "The New Reality in Motivation." WOW! I was sabotaging my own efforts. I had purchased a gun, purchased bullets, taken careful aim and shot myself in the foot – repeatedly.

Dr. Callahan challenges our belief system about what will work and what will not work in motivating our singers. There was a time, in the postwar culture of the '50s, when social conformity allowed leaders to motivate based on challenge, reasonability, and commitment. Even through the decades to follow, including the radical '60s all the way through the "me" generation (whichever one that really is), these efforts tended to have some results.

But no more.

Dr. Callahan proceeds to describe Motivational Fuels prioritizing them in the following order:

1. **Compassion:** sharing, caring, giving, loving, serving
2. **Community:** roots, place, belonging, family, friends
3. **Challenge:** attain, accomplish, achieve
4. **Reasonability:** data, logic, analysis, good sense
5. **Commitment:** loyalty, duty, obligation

By first reminding them of their commitment, I had started at the complete wrong end of the list trying to motivate (badger) my chorus members into compliance.

When you ask singers or instrumentalists why they are in choir (or band or orchestra), it frequently starts with, "I like the people in the choir," "I thought it would be a great place to find a 'family' and develop friends," "I love music and rather than just perform by myself, I wanted to join with others to create something larger than I could ever do alone."

None of these people were going to say, "I needed something that would absorb my life, my money, my free time, my every waking moment." And, sadly, you never hear, "I just wanted to be in your presence as many hours a week as possible."

First, our singers want to share something with the world. They want to find a safe place to do that. They want a place where they can feel they belong and music provides that team sport for them. As they grow, they become challenged by the goals set before them. At that point, we can appeal to their minds about reaching more people if we work a little harder "raising the bar" to build the program. When they have bought all of that, and only then, do they formulate a deep sense of commitment to what we do

47

Of course we have those angels sent from on high who join and are simply committed from the first breath. God bless them – and make them fruitful and multiply!

It's a Choir! It's a Family! It's a Support Group!

Sounds like multiple personality disorder. But at any given moment, your chorus is all of the above and more! You may be the one to choose the order and the appearance of the different personalities, but sometimes these things are chosen for you. Never forget singing in a choir is a vehicle for socialization and social change.

Humanist psychologist Abraham Maslow has formulated a theory of the needs hierarchy of humans. Most astounding is that seven of the eight basic needs of humans are covered by singing in a chorus!

1. **Biological** (food, drink, rest, oxygen, etc.)
2. **Safety** (create a place of safety and trust)
3. **Attachment** (with you, with each other, with listeners)
4. **Esteem** (pride in accomplishment)
5. **Cognitive** (making music improves I.Q.)
6. **Aesthetic** (art lifts everyone to a higher level)
7. **Self-actualization** (getting in touch with inner self)
8. **Spiritual** (sharing and giving of self)

There is no activity people can engage in that meets as many basic human needs as being in a choir.

This is a huge responsibility for you. There are few other experiences your singers can have that so thoroughly meet their many-faceted life needs. And if you have an occasional potluck, you can take care of #1 and hit all 8 of them!

Why do they sing for you? Because they trust you.

Take a moment and go back to a point in your own life when you gave yourself over to a conductor completely. You already identified this in the self-assessment questionnaire earlier in the book. What made you turn over your control mechanism to this person? What was that experience like for you? Have you been able to replicate it now that you are the conductor? If you have not, then you are most likely not letting go enough of your own emotions and connecting with your singers. You are not instilling in them the ability to trust you completely. Perhaps this is because you are not completely confident you can take them to the destination you have planned for them. They will sense this every time. Have confidence. Ask them to trust you. And when you ask, make very sure you are ready in every way to protect their trust and make their investment well worth their while.

Every time your chorus sings, it takes a risk.

There is a risk that they might not do their best or reach their potential. There is a risk of being embarrassed in public.
There is always that risk that they might blurt out an unscheduled solo.

Singing is a very vulnerable thing to do. Polls have ranked things people fear most in their lives and have come up with death as #1 and public speaking as #2. And surely singing in public would be right there at the top of the list if it were one of the choices. Certainly it is much more of a risk than, say, being on a bowling team. You can always blame poor performance on the shoes, the lanes or your bowling ball!

Remember:
They trust you.
Trust is earned.
Trust is also fragile.

They trust you to teach them, direct them, protect them and lead them in doing something they could never do on their own.

They trust that you will respect them and the gift of their time and talent and use it wisely.

They trust that you will not embarrass, humiliate or abuse them when they open themselves up to you.

Yes, many will impose other roles on you: father, mother, brother, sister, pastor, etc. These are not in the job description or your responsibility. Only you are in control of how many of these added duties you are willing to accept. Warning: if you accept them, no complaining later.

The roles of conductor, mentor, teacher, and guide are automatically yours. When they put their unqualified trust in you, when they stand before you and share with you one of the most vulnerable experiences of their lives, it is both your love for the music you are making and respect for the gift of trust in you that will ultimately change both of your lives. And that of your listeners as well.

Is it a free ride for the passengers or do they help along the way?

Tony Thornton has written a comprehensive book from the singers' point of view called *The Choral Singer's Survival Guide*. In it, he lists the responsibilities of the singers (travelers). Some of them are:

1. Coming to rehearsal with your notes and rhythms learned
2. Active listening
3. A beautiful tone on every note
4. Exact intonation on every note
5. Beautiful phrasing
6. Intelligible diction on each and every syllable
7. To communicate the music through an engaged mind, body, and spirit
8. To work as a team player with the other members of your chorus.

This is fantastic information! It is far from a free ride.

How do you get them to come along on the journey?

Everyone asks about recruitment. Everyone thinks member recruitment simply lies in the advertising. It has to be flyers and announcements and even ads in the local papers. (Have you heard that before?) This is not the case.

First, have a clearly defined mission/vision statement for the chorus. They need to know exactly what they are signing on to do and the parameters. They certainly must have a membership manual that describes all of the expectations. Another idea is to have the mission statement of the group on a sign in the front of every rehearsal every week.

One of the most telling graphics using the circles is one that has helped me understand why some people just aren't going to ever be happy in one of my choruses, no matter how hard I try.

The first circle represents my chorus. It is who we are and what we stand for through our music. It is not going to change a great deal.

There are those perfect members whose motivation for singing intersects multiple aspects of the chorus. Maybe it is that person who truly understands the life-changing potential of music.

Then there are the problem singers:

1. One of the biggest problems arises when a person singing in your ensemble has a purpose for singing that is far from that of the chorus. For example, if a person only shares the desire to entertain all of the time and is mostly in your chorus just to be in the spotlight, this is a problem. This person shares none of the altruistic principles upon which the chorus thrives.

2. There is also the person who does not agree with any of the principles but is simply looking for a social outlet.

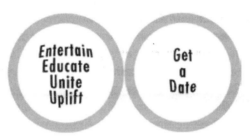

3. There is also the person who wants to change the course of the organization from the outside.

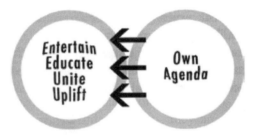

A close second in recruitment is what I call the "buzz." This is the "water cooler" or the "coffee room" talk. Member recruitment is internal and organic – not so much external. You can put signs all over town and ads in every paper about auditions, but it is what your singers are saying to their friends that really matters.

If rehearsals aren't fun, well planned, and enjoyable, you'll never get more singers. Trust me, your singers talk outside rehearsal (and you thought they only talked during rehearsal!). When they leave rehearsal, if they are saying "that is the most fun part of my week," others will want to join them. Imagine, however, them saying "that is the longest, most boring, useless hour of my week....why don't you join us?"

If your singers are saying, "I can't wait until Tuesday night. It is the most fun, productive evening of my entire week," who wouldn't want to join them to see what it is about. If your singers are saying, "Oh, dear, tonight's rehearsal and I'd rather have a root canal," who is going to even give it a consideration?

For your singers, you are only as good as your NEXT concert.

For your audience, you are only as good as your LAST concert.

What does that mean? Well, your audience only remembers your last concert. This determines whether they would like to attend another concert! For your singers, they forget the last one very quickly, even as soon as you pass out the music for the next concert! They are only going to continue to be engaged depending on whether or not they "like" or are "moved by" or are "challenged by" the next concert you have chosen. They will not rest long on the laurels of the last concert.

Audience Development

Just as member recruitment, everyone thinks that audience development simply lies in the advertising. This is not the case.

Number one key: consistency of product!

Give five great concerts in a row, no one mentions it, not to your friends or theirs. Give ten great concerts in a row, they will be permanent fans and start talking. Give one bad concert, they'll stay away for the next five and tell all their friends.

Invite some surprise fellow travelers along by going outside the box and creating new and exciting partnerships.

One of the most rewarding experiences you and your chorus will have is when you think outside the box in programming and in collaborations. Regardless of whether you are in a church, school or community chorus, there are opportunities galore just waiting for you. Whether that is in collaboration with dancers, instrumentalists, actors, children, or ethnic music groups and on and on. You and your singers and your audience will only be enriched by these kinds of events. Yes, it takes time and energy. But the payoff is worth it.

Use your imagination. Use your creativity. Just because everyone you know is taking the family on a prepackaged generic vacation to a popular theme park for three nights, four days, breakfast buffet included, doesn't mean you have to!

Just because your colleagues are all doing cookie-cutter concerts singing all of the repertoire in chronological order, selecting one group from each musical time period, that doesn't mean you have to!

Why should we do this? What is the payoff?

The answer seems obvious. When we have stretched outside our comfort zone, the results have always been absolutely remarkable. It is so "second nature" to us that anything else is foreign.

A few years ago, we sponsored a Cochlear Implant Children's Choir in conjunction with the Callier Institute for Communication Disorders. They joined us on stage with 50 other hearing impaired students.   We, and the audience, were changed. On three different occasions, we have joined with a 100-voice African American chorus from the First Baptist Church of Hamilton Park, a suburb of Dallas. Singing with over 300 men on stage, in a cross-cultural experience was wonderful. We have performed with local dance troupes, instrumental ensembles, etc. It deepens your own singers' experience in addition to audience development, goodwill, P.R., etc. You have the same type of opportunities in your own school, church or community chorus. You just have to allow yourself and those around you to create them.

In a commencement speech to Julliard graduates, playwright Terrence McNally had these important words to say.

"You can be a safe artist or a dangerous one. There's room for both of them. The only thing you cannot be is a dishonest one. The first job of an artist is to tell the truth. When we are dishonest in our work, we stop being artists and become instead that most dreaded of words: a hack. And what is the point in being dishonest in our work as artists? We are always found out. Always. We never get away with it. Conveying it honestly, we connect with our fellow human beings who cannot articulate in their daily lives what we can in our songs, our dances, our plays, our music and [those] who hunger for beauty in their lives as surely as a plant needs water and sun.

"When you think and act and live like an artist, you are never alone. Never. There is always someone else out there. Always. You may not know that, but they're there and they are grateful to you that you played, that you sang, that you danced just for them."

PART TWO: Hitting the Road
Rehearsals Begin

Buckle Your Seat Belts

Start Your Engines

TMI and TLC

Vocal Health

Expect Detours!

Maintaining Control

Arriving on Time

The Warm-up Before the Performance

Chapter 9

Buckle Your Seat Belts
"Are we there yet?"

Before you put the car in gear, everything should be in order. There should be gas in the car and the oil and tire pressure checked. You might even wash it! The packing list should be checked and everyone should be engaged and fresh for the journey. Everything should be in order. No excuses allowed at that point.

In the same vein, the beginning of each concert session should be organized within an inch of its life. My suggestion is that you start each concert session with the singers having their music in the order of the concert, not some random order such as alphabetical. If you are conducting a church choir, then the folders should be organized in the order in which the anthems will be sung as the weeks progress.

This may seem a departure from what most of you have been taught, but it has certainly worked for us. From the very beginning of the rehearsal period for a concert, you at least have an idea of what you think the order of the concert will be. Begin with the concert order in your mind and in their music packet from the very get-go. This alone makes rehearsals go more smoothly as they are not constantly searching for the next piece. It also has a great deal with how I organize rehearsals. A few times in the rehearsal period, you can go in reverse order, just to make sure you learn that final song!

We learned from our college days that we were best when we sang through our recital many times, in order, before the actual performance date. This has to do with pacing of the voice and is equally important in a choral program. The singers (and you) need to know what the demands of the program are going to be far in advance of the actual concert. You may think this sounds crazy, but it will help you in every possible way imaginable. You may find that two of the songs you put back to back really don't work. You may discover a segue or relationship between songs you might have overlooked. And you have plenty of time to change them.

Are We There Yet?

Depending on how well your chorus sight-reads, you may be able to sing through all of the pieces on the very first rehearsal and achieve as much as 60 percent of what you are hoping for by the time the performance comes along. If you continue to work on small parts of most or all of the pieces, then the next week you will be at 65 percent. The next week it will get a little better and by the time the performance takes place, you may be at 90 percent for the entire concert and even 95 percent on some pieces.

Working on one piece for an entire rehearsal, or even most of one, may mean you get to 90 percent accuracy on that song, that week. But you left all of the other pieces at 60 percent. By skipping a week and not rehearsing them, they will probably slip to 55 or 50 percent the next time you sing them. At this rate, your concert is going to be horribly out of balance. You will have a few pieces that are great and a few that are horrible, because you spent all of your time on only a few.

And don't forget that if you have one rehearsal a week, or even two, you can spend a great deal of time getting one piece to 95 percent, but your singers will come back the next week at 75 percent on that song. All of the pieces you have selected (and that remain throughout the rehearsal period) are your children. They need equal treatment. Otherwise, why did you choose them? Surely not as filler.

Start and Finish

Begin your rehearsal in the most positive way possible. How about starting by singing something easy in the repertoire they are working on, with specific attention to a vocal concept, and saving your actual warm-ups for 10 minutes into the rehearsal? There is certainly no harm done in that – occasionally.

Plan the end of rehearsal as carefully as the beginning so you end on the same positive, energetic note on which you started. Don't just run out of time while you are in the middle of note-chasing with the basses.

When you have worked the horses hard in the field and the day is over, you head them for the barn and LET THEM GO. The same is true of your singers. You work them hard. At the end of a long work session, head them for the barn and let them sing! Save the last minutes of your rehearsal to just let them sing. Singing is why they are here!

They may have already packed the mental satchel and are not going to learn anything of substance the last 10 minutes anyway, so have some fun and let 'er rip! Select the last song you sing carefully. They will be humming it for days and either be thanking or cursing you.

The Dreaded Middle of the Trip

The monotony of a long drive can be dangerous and can put you to sleep at the wheel! Were you ever driving along and somehow "woke up" and were much farther down the road than you thought, not remembering having covered miles in the journey? It's not just daydreaming – it is very dangerous. I once heard a person say the hardest thing for them to do while teaching was to stay awake! How sad for the students.

Remember those long car trips and family vacations? Playing those car games like "I spy with my little eye," "Ninety-nine bottles of soda on the wall," etc. Well, that was before we were spoiled by flying everywhere for vacation (or for choir tours). But you certainly remember how much fun they were – for the first hour. And less fun as the hours progressed. While we have many tools that can make our process of preparing music easier, we do not have something like a jet airplane to get us from square one to a polished concert in just three hours! If I could think of that, I would be rich!

The most important thing you can do in planning your rehearsals is to make sure you do not fall into that "I spy" monotone, humdrum of predictability.

A.D.D.

We live in a fast-paced world. Everything we do is fast-paced. We are accustomed to multi-tasking with information coming at us all at once from many directions. It is the way we are, period. You can't fight that. And it has resulted in a great deal of attention deficits all around the room. For this reason, and several others, my suggestion is to divide your rehearsal in five-minute increments on your rehearsal planning sheet. As you will see from the sample plan on page 63, there may be a piece you want to spend 15 minutes on. If so, you must consciously mark through three of your five-minute increments.

They need to know you have a plan. They don't need to know what it is.

Rehearsal Plan

One of our most difficult and sometimes time-consuming tasks is to make rehearsal plans. It is one of the things that we sometimes let fall by the wayside when crunch time comes. We think perhaps other things take precedence, but that is a thought pattern that needs reversing.

Make a rehearsal plan template for your computer. Fill it in for each rehearsal. Save them all! This is one way you can continue to swap out your warm-ups to keep them interesting and applicable to the repertoire you are singing.

The first thing that needs to be on your rehearsal plan and at the top of your mind are your goals for that rehearsal. Without specific goals, you can never feel you have truly accomplished anything.

There are many varied opinions about what should be done with the rehearsal plan once it is made. Many of you believe it should be put on a board in front of the chorus or passed out to them. My opinion is that this is not a good idea. You may want to change your mind midstream. You need to have the freedom to spend longer on one piece if it needs it and adjust the schedule as you go along. You may also like the freedom to skip a piece. If you continually show them your plan and change your mind too often, they won't think you plan very efficiently in the first place.

Blackboard or no blackboard? This is a question that has everything to do with your own planning and rehearsal style. It also has to do with what kind of chorus you are conducting and how often they meet. For me, it works much better for my singers to have their music in concert order in their notebooks. For example, right now they have two concerts and a recording in their notebook(s). I also do not want them to have to rearrange their music or their notebooks each week according to my rehearsal plan. We rehearse in concert order.

Do share the plan with your accompanists and musical section leaders and anyone else that might have something to do with the rehearsal. The entire process then goes much more smoothly.

A conducting student came in recently and stated proudly that he had prepared so incredibly well for his community chorus rehearsal that he had managed to spend an entire hour and a half rehearsing one song!

I congratulated him and told him the proof of his expertise would be clearly demonstrated the next week when half of his singers stayed home! But they luckily gave him the benefit of the doubt. They knew he was green and showed up the next week to give him another chance. He had actually done a rehearsal plan in five-minute increments. He was much happier as were his singers.

Do not make them sit through too much note-chasing. If possible, the ideal situation is to never chase notes when the full chorus is present. If that is not practical, at least never have one section of the choir spend too much time on one portion of the music while the others simply sit idly by. It can only serve to defeat them musically and kill the morale. Find a way to divide them into sections to pound out notes. If you have to chase notes for one section, allow the others to lightly hum their parts as the section in question sings theirs.

Halfway through rehearsal, go back and repeat or pick a new exercise for breathing, relaxation or one that has to do with the repertoire you have chosen for the last part of rehearsal. For heaven's sake, if you do an exercise at the beginning that relates to a piece you have scheduled to rehearse an hour later, they won't remember it.

Instant Clinic (with no fee for clinician)

Divide and conquer. Divide your chorus into half, regardless of how small or large, and have one half perform a piece for the other half. They will invariably be tougher on each other than you ever would be. When the second group performs, the "judges" are then compelled to perform and demonstrate all of the things they corrected in the first group.

Circle the room with quartets or octets. Then go around the room and allow each small group to sing – as if passing off a baton to each other. This will really show all of the singers where the most work is needed.

Daily Grind

At a recent workshop, a public school director came up to me and said, "most of what you are saying is for a once or twice a week rehearsal. I have each of my choirs five days a week – 60 minutes a day. What can I do to keep rehearsals fresh and alive?" He has his choir for five hours a week. I have my choir for five or six hours a week. The answer is the same: Plan, plan, plan. Variety is the spice of life. You will only become boring if you think you can "wing it."

Make a grid of the five one-hour rehearsals in a week. Look at the variety of things you can possibly do as well as the wide range of activities you have to do to keep the group going. At that point, mix it up! Keep them guessing. They need to look forward to coming to choir each day or three times a week or whatever because they don't know exactly what will happen during rehearsal – except that they are going to get to sing together, make some great music, and have a lot of fun in the process.

They don't need to know that at every choir rehearsal the following will happen and in this order:

1. Attendance will be taken
2. There will be 10 minutes of warm-ups (the same every time)
3. They will sing the same songs in the same order, trying to fix the same things, every rehearsal.
4. They will be dodging notes and rests and rhythms for the next 30 minutes.
5. There will be announcements about the fund-raising, costuming, and selling tickets.
6. They will be told they are behind the preparation schedule and "Have a nice day."

Trading Spaces

Sometimes you have to change the place you rehearse. Singing is kinesthetic, based on muscle memory. Your singers can only reproduce sounds when they "remember" the correct feel of them. They must know that the sound they make in one rehearsal location is the same at a different rehearsal location – and the same in the performance facility. Your job is to make any adjustments for a new location, not theirs.

RETREAT (used as a noun, not a command)

One of the most beneficial things any of us can do is to have retreats with our choruses. These can be an "in-town" one-day retreat or even a weekend "get-away." Of course, you youngsters can have all-night "Lock-ins," although singing at 3:30 a.m. is not my definition of a good time! When we go on retreat, we work very hard. An in-town retreat is normally from 10:00 a.m. to 5:00 p.m. and is very useful. On our out of town retreats, we are able to get in 10 - 12 hours of hard work into rehearsals and at least that much into play and bonding exercises. Such events are invaluable to you in your rehearsal plans.

Don't's and Do's

Some Don'ts and Do's of Rehearsal
(add your own and laminate it for your office wall!)

Don't start late.
> **Do** have someone ready to begin rehearsal for you.

Don't begin by talking too much.
> **Do** begin by allowing them to move, stretch, massage, etc.

Don't lose focus between every piece of music.
> **Do** stick to your plan – think ahead!

Don't talk about every piece. (TMI!)
> **Do** plan which pieces to discuss and which ones can wait.

Don't spend too much time chasing notes with one section.
> **Do** that in sectionals or divide them some way.

Don't spend too much time on one piece ignoring the others.
> **Do** treat each piece with equal attention.

Don't allow for too many announcements.
> **Do** have written notes and one person make announcements.

Don't end rehearsal by talking.
> **Do** choose the final piece wisely.

Don't end on the most difficult piece.
> **Do** send them off singing, humming, smiling and they will return doing the same!

All the above will absolutely KILL the flow of rehearsal. The whole point is to take your singers on a musical journey through all of their emotions. This journey is one that is planned by you, carefully It's like leaving on a nice family vacation and stopping at every rest stop, truck stop, and historical marker. YOU WILL NEVER GET WHERE YOU ARE HEADED, you'll be too exhausted from the starts and stops!

Rehearsal Plan

Goals tonight:

_____

_____

_____

Have fun.

Rehearsal (in concert order)
7:30 Warm-ups – chosen from 5 categories
7:35 Warm-ups – taken from specific repertoire
7:40
7:45
7:50
7:55
8:00
8:05
8:10
8:15
8:20
8:25
8:30 Announcements
8:35 Mini-break
8:40 Warm down exercise
8:45
8:50
8:55
9:00
9:05
MEMORY WORK: stand and sing
9:10
9:15
9:20
9:25 Sing their favorite song

Good night – a few minutes early makes them think you are the best, most organized conductor in the world.

63

Musical Mishaps
Time-savers

Another incredible tool we use is the "Musical Mishap" form. It is a small form that we take to the local copy place and have made into tear-off pads. These are placed in the back of the room. Most singers have one in their notebook, just in case. With two hundred-plus singers, we would never get through a single rehearsal if each person raised their hand just one time to ask for a note to be played or a rhythm to be clarified. We have sectionals to learn notes. We don't learn notes in the full chorus rehearsals.

But occasionally, sectionals just aren't enough. That is where the form comes in. If a person sitting in the middle of a section notices that they are not getting a passage, rather than raise his/her hand, they fill out the Musical Mishap form and turn it in to the musical section leader or to the conductor. This allows me to go through the forms before the next rehearsal. I will either make a list of all of them and hit them all at the beginning of rehearsal, or will write them in my rehearsal plan so that when we get to that piece, we hit that section first.

You cannot imagine how much time it saves and how great your chorus feels that you have addressed their "issues." A form is provided on the next page.

Musical Mishaps

Please circle the appropriate section:

S	A	T	B
(T1)	(T2)	(Bar.)	(Bass)

Title of song _____

Measures of concern _____

What is the problem? (notes, rhythm, tone)

_____

_____

_____

_____

Please return to any of the following:
Conductor, Assistant Conductor, Accompanist,
Musical Section Leader
Or
E-mail to the conductor.

Thank you very much for your input!

Chapter 10

Start Your Engines!
The Warm-Ups!!

By now, everyone knows I am completely focused on vocal technique and warming up a chorus, so, this question comes up all the time: "How long should you spend warming up your chorus?" My answer: "However long your rehearsal is!" You should never stop listening critically to the sound your chorus is making. And you should never hesitate to stop and deal with sounds that are not pleasing or appropriate to the repertoire. If you think, "I'll fix that next week," the danger is you won't get around to it then, either. After awhile, your singers wonder if you even notice.

Every time your chorus meets, you must do at least one exercise from each of the following groups and in the following order. Of course, you are more than welcome to do more than one from each, if you have time. But you <u>must</u> do one from each group – every time – and not skip a single one; nor take them out of order.

Appetizer – Posture
Soup – Breathing
Salad – Phonation
Entrée – Resonance
Dessert – Blend!

Preparing your chorus to sing is one of the most important things a choral director can do. The difficulty lies in the fact that you have 20 or 200 people in front of you, each of whom is in a different state of readiness to sing and each of whom has a different level of experience. Your task is to find the middle ground from which all can benefit. This is an enormous challenge.

Start with Big Muscle Groups and Work Down.

Singing should be an athletic endeavor. After all, when done properly, it involves the entire body. There is no other athletic event where a person arrives and simply begins playing. Everyone begins with stretching. If you hire a trainer, they will always begin by having you stretch before moving to the big muscle groups. Most often, these are lunges!

What do we do as trainers of vocal athletes? We get our singers in a room, have them sit down, and start with the smallest muscle possible – the vocal folds! This trend simply must be reversed. Warm-ups must begin with the individual's needs, starting with the big muscle groups, getting the body awake, stretching, etc., and only then moving to other tasks at hand.

TAKE NOTE! "Never do a vocalise unless you know the WHY."

When I conduct workshops with other choruses, I tell the singers that they should never do a warm-up for which they do not know the purpose. They are encouraged to respectfully raise their hands and ask the conductor what a particular exercise is supposed to teach them. This sometimes causes great consternation for conductors whose only answer is "because my high school choir teacher used it." It also causes those to sweat who either never thought of the "why" or who are just using the exercises as a "filler" or to kill time. "Killing time" is not an answer I would suggest you use, regardless of how true it might be.

Perhaps you've heard the old adage, "Never try to teach a pig to sing. It wastes your time and annoys the pig."

Unfortunately, we do waste a lot of time. Go through all of your books, papers, and notes from high school, college, and your teaching career. Gather together all of the warm-ups you have written down. Then sit down and make a list of all the warm-ups you can ever remember doing. Put them in one place. Look at them. Sort them. Categorize them according to the five groups on the previous page. Most importantly, decide how each one of them builds vocal or choral technique, so you can answer that pesky singer who wants to know why they are being asked to do this exercise.

You are the only voice teacher most of your singers will ever have!

Warming Up

Are your muscles stiff when you get up in the morning? Well, so are your vocal folds. They are like Silly Putty taken out of the freezer! They have had drainage oozing over them all night, or even worse, have been completely dried up by heated or refrigerated air blowing on them all night. They have not phonated in 8 to 12 hours. You can take the Silly Putty out of the freezer and warm it slowly in your hands. You can't take your folds out and massage them, but they still need it for the gymnastics you are about to ask them to do. Stretching your muscles actually focuses blood flow to them, thereby raising the temperature of the muscles. You cannot begin the day without appropriate warm-ups. Doing so will eventually cause damage to your instrument: hemorrhaging, blisters or even worse, the dreaded nodes.

The First Three Courses

Appetizer. Begin by getting all of your singers' bodies engaged in the process. Get the blood flowing. Jog, bend, stretch, windmill, massage, Hokey Pokey, sternum power…you need to be creative here.

Soup. Then get their breathing mechanism engaged. Work on extending the breath lower and deeper than in normal breathing. Use the air elevator, Farinelli, inner-tube. You name it, they'll do it.

Salad. Only after you have their attention, their bodies' attention, and their breathing mechanism's attention may you even ponder adding vocal folds and allowing them to utter a sound!

And you MUST be gentle when you begin to engage them. This means that when you begin to add the vocal folds, you do it gently, avoiding singing too loudly or with a tight or hyperfunctional mechanism. This is achieved by engaging the breath mechanism fully and using the bumble bee or blowing your finger while singing. Always pay close attention to an easy onset of the tone, shying away from glottal attacks.

In an article from 2001 in the National Association of Teachers of Singing's *Journal of Singing*, world-renowned voice scientist Dr. Ingo Titze lists his five favorite vocal warm-ups. In it, his very first suggestion is the lip trill. Some reasons he lists are: engaging respiratory muscles quickly; minimizing force on vocal folds; spreading the vocal folds so that only the edges are vibrating; and lowering the phonation threshold.

The issue here is "breath-pacing," not "breath support." These are completely different concepts. Once your singers have a good knowledge of the breathing mechanism, it is then up to them, or you, how to use that breath in free phonation.

If you are having an evening rehearsal, you don't need a warm-up as much as a...

Warming Down

Your singers have been talking all day at work, school or at home. Their vocal folds do not resemble cold Silly Putty at all. In fact, they are well warmed up. Your task is to "warm them down," not up. The Silly Putty is pliable already. Their vocal folds are warmed up (at least in the lower range) and don't need as much of your attention as they would in the morning hours.

The beginning goals of warming down are similar to those of warming up: posture and breathing. Beyond that, once vocal folds are added, the main focus is range extension, because even though they have most likely been talking all day, it is only in the lower registers. The majority of people speak much too low for many reasons. The men want to sound like "manly men," and women also have the impression that speaking low makes them sound assertive and smart – as opposed to the dumb blonde or Betty Boop syndrome.

Once we have our singers using perfect posture, breathing perfectly, and using free-flowing phonation throughout their range, we can move to the final areas of resonance, articulation, and blend.

Here is a plan you can use for every rehearsal to help you plan the order of your warm-ups and also keep them fresh.

5-Course Meal of Warm-Ups

Select One per Group:

Appetizer – Posture:

_____

(shoulder rubs, shaking out, jogging in place)

Soup – Breathing:

_____

(no vocal fold involvement)

Salad – Phonation:

_____

(attack, range extension, freedom)

Entrée – Resonators:

_____

(work on vowels, tone color, articulation)

Dessert – Artistry:

Do - Re - Mi - Fa - So - Fa - Mi - Re - Do

(choral blend)

①   ②   ③   ④

In your plan, create some warm-ups from specific pieces you will be singing during the evening. Certainly you can (and should) choose more than one from some groups; just don't completely leave any out, or you'll go away hungry.

Also select a couple for after break or later in the rehearsal.

Warning: You can kill vocal technique by beginning every rehearsal with sight-reading.

Do your sight-reading in carefully planned, short sprints! Once you begin sight-reading, your chorus turns all of its attention to the intervals, rhythms, etc. and takes their minds off the freedom of the vocal apparatus you have worked for the last 10 or 20 minutes to achieve. Practice your sight-reading throughout the rehearsal, rather than in one big chunk.

"But why can't I just let the chorus warm up on our repertoire? We don't really have time to devote to warm-ups."

You can never teach your chorus to sing by using repertoire. Period.

When we sing repertoire, we bring too many distractions and issues to the actual singing. We bring idiosyncrasies of language and emotional attachment to the music. The focus is then divided among words, rhythms, dynamics, and a million things unrelated to vocal development.

I am a huge proponent of using repertoire to create warm-ups. However, it requires a great deal of work and planning on your part. There are two ways to do this. One is for you to sit down in advance of your rehearsal and select portions of the music that you feel might be a challenge, or portions that you think make good warm-ups. Isolate these and select the vocal concepts you wish to teach by using them. One of the great rewards of doing this is that when your singers get to those selections, they automatically remember the concept you taught them.

The other way to achieve this is for you to actually LISTEN to the way they are singing during rehearsal. Of course this requires you to take some of your focus away from the notes, the rhythms, the dynamics, etc. and just listen to the sound. As they sing, you are then required to be able to think of vocalises on the fly. This is sometimes the best way to teach concepts because then the singers realize that vocalizing is not something abstract and unrelated to actual singing. This is where the absolutely crucial concept of diagnosis and prescription comes into play.

It is no coincidence that the first two syllables of REHEARSAL are
RE HEAR!
You must RE HEAR your choir every time they open their mouths!

Diagnosis

We are all very good at diagnosing issues when listening to other choruses. But not always so objective about our own, or, most importantly, how to go about fixing ours (or others for that matter). Imagine this. You are sitting with a friend in the audience at a choral concert. As the chorus sings, you begin to think of what they are doing wrong. The minute you have that thought, the lights immediately come up, a voice comes from above and says, "So, you thought they were singing out of tune (or too bright or their vowels didn't match or whatever)?" You sheepishly say, "Yes, I did." At that point a microphone drops down right in front of you and the voice says, "Fix it!"

Well, that puts a new perspective on your thought processes the next time you go to someone else' concert. We all know how to diagnose, but may not know what to prescribe for the problem.

There is another indication that you not have honed the skill of diagnosis. If your chorus gets the same comments every year, whether at contest or reviews, you may not know how to fix what's wrong. There are only so many years you can blame poor judging or crazy reviewers before you simply have to look at what it is you are doing. So, once the problem has been diagnosed, you need the…

Prescription

All too often, we don't know exactly what to do, so we address problems that have nothing to do with the root causes. For example, if your chorus is singing out of tune, the first place not to begin is with "placement in the mask." It is all the way back to the beginning – check their posture, then their breathing. Make sure they are using free phonation. Then and only then, can you start worrying about adjusting the resonance patterns they are using. You can tweak all you want – have them raise their eyebrows until they disappear into their hairlines – but if they do not know how to stand or how to breathe, it will be for naught.

Your chorus must also be able to **hear** the difference themselves when you diagnose a problem and prescribe a method for change. They must also be able to **feel** the difference in how they produce what you are asking them to change. At that point, they have three options:

1. Understand and like/accept the change you are requesting. This would be getting the prescription filled immediately.

2. Trust that you know what you're doing even if they don't like it or even understand it. Wait a few days to think about it before getting the prescription filled.

3. Find another chorus to join – or another hobby. Get a second opinion from another conductor.

Teach concepts, not clones

One of the important concepts for us as choral conductors is that we are not in the business of making the singers in our choruses sound like us. When we demonstrate for them, we must convey the vocal concept, not the actual sound they are hearing. We must model technique and ask them to internalize and incorporate the concept, not mimic our sound. You are not the only one who needs to understand the concept behind the example. If they are to learn technique from you, they must know this. The worst example of teachers who do not understand this concept are the ones whose students can't warm up on their own or know why they are even doing it!

As you know, we conductors sometimes have the strangest gestures that get amazing results from our choruses. These gestures may have nothing to do with the sound but, because we have taught them through words and repetition what a particular gesture means, our singers are able to replicate the sound we have described rather than the sound we are demonstrating with our gesture.

The same is true of conductors when they are teaching vocal technique. We repeat what we were taught with little factual or descriptive support. But we may demonstrate a particular sound or action that goes along with words that are meaningless.

Be careful what you say!

In our profession, we must always be conscious of the fact that the things we say to our singers become truth for them. As you know, there are many people who don't think they can sing simply because at some point in their lives, someone either told them they couldn't or maybe even gave them a disparaging look when they did. The scars can last a lifetime.

Our corrective comments must never be at the expense of an individual. If you are having difficulty with one singer in your chorus, you owe it to him/her to discuss it in private. Pointing it out in front of the chorus is the wrong way to go about getting the results you want. But continually browbeating an entire section, in the hopes that the one person will hear your message, is also fruitless in most cases. They seldom think you are talking to them!

All too often, we simply repeat instructions we were taught with little or no examination as to whether it has basis in actual truth. These statements have become commonplace in our art. We accompany our ridiculous statements with a demonstration of exactly what it is we wish them to accomplish. This goes back to teaching clones, not concepts. So, we use words that have no real meaning, but when coupled with a demonstration we wish them to mimic, the end result is somewhat successful.

There are several problems inherent in this:

1. They really haven't learned anything but notes, rhythm, words, and technique by rote.
2. When they sing in someone else's chorus, they have to relearn vocal/choral technique and an entire new vocabulary and language.
3. They might very well have their own chorus one day and will simply pass on the instructions without truly understanding the concept behind it.
4. Your chorus will sound just like you. Perhaps you sing beautifully, but when you are not there to warm them up and demonstrate for them, they will be lost.

If you have said any of the following, please get out your vocal pedagogy or voice science books and try to discover the physiological basis for your instruction. Even if your suggestions are purely empirical, they should be founded in good vocal technique.

Here are some of my favorites:

Focus the tone!
What does that mean? Is that a phonation issue (breathy) or a resonance issue (spread) or a color issue (white)?

Support with the diaphragm!
That can't be done, regardless of how many times you have heard that said or said it yourself.

Place the tone in the mask.
You may as well say place the tone on a platter and garnish with parsley.

Take some weight off your cords!
If most of us knew how to take weight off just because someone told us to, we certainly would.

Blend, you rascals!
They have no idea what that means except to cut back and basically stop singing.

Don't just let that note sit there, make it go somewhere.
And where did you want it to go? Next door, or down the street?

Raising the eyebrows while singing will improve the tone quality.
There is absolutely no basis for this. It will not help tuning and it looks terrible.

Richard Miller, one of the world's leading voice scientists and vocal pedagogues has his own list that he shares in his book *On the Art of Singing*. Read this and see if you have ever used them in your instruction.

Pull in the diaphragm to give "support" for the high notes.

Drop the chest to avoid high-chest breathing.

Concentrate on center of the forehead so that the tone will be placed "up and over."

Flare the nostrils to "open the throat" and increase the resonance of the voice.

Throw the tone to the back of the hall.

Place the tone in the frontal sinuses.

All of the above examples are taken from pedagogic sources. These technical maneuvers hold place in some pedagogies because they seem as though they ought to be true. They are not what they seem.

Factual information in no way hinders artistic imagination.

Video-record an entire rehearsal, especially when you are spending time on choral/vocal technique. While viewing it, see if you can fully explain every single thing you have said to the singers.

Chapter 11

TMI and TLC in Rehearsal
"Do we have to stop at EVERY historical marker?"

There are many layers involved in preparing a piece of music before you introduce it to your singers. One of the most important things the conductor must do is to study the piece thoroughly. Then he/she must decide how much of that information is important to have simply studied and how much of it the singers really need to know. Certainly the singers will be impressed by your studious care with the music. Mostly they just want to sing. A good practice is to share bits of the information as you go along in the rehearsal process. DON'T TALK TOO MUCH!

A singer once told me that at a recent rehearsal of his chorus, the conductor talked through the entire two and a half hour rehearsal. She told them why she chose the music and the background material of each piece. The chorus sat patiently with the music in their hands. At the end of the two and a half hours, she said she was sorry they didn't get to sing any of the music, but it would just heighten their anticipation for the next week. WRONG.

There are obviously many things you need to look at before your chorus ever sings a note. A few of those are:

Key signature: key changes; meter; meter changes; dynamic peaks and valleys.

Horizontal movement: wide or difficult leaps; boring lines; mark beats when difficult.

Vertical relationships: interesting harmonic changes; find foundation; sing from bottom up.

Difficult entrances: What cues will they need? What vocal instruction? Where will they find their pitch?

Breathing issues: Where are the breaths? Where are the long phrases with staggered breathing?

Tone quality: What does the time period or the style of the piece require?

Consonants: Where are the difficult ones? Which ones might not be heard? Which ones may cause difficulty?

The text: Speak the text in rhythm. Who wrote it? When and why?

What is TMI for your chorus?

How much of this information do your singers really need? Some might want all of it; some don't want to be bothered with any of it. After you have done all of this for yourself, decide how much you should share with your chorus. My experience is that the more well-trained and educated the singers, the less they really want to hear.

Only you can really know what your singers can handle in the way of information. Once you have done your homework, go back and select what you think is truly interesting; what sets this piece apart from all of the others; and what part of the information will truly make a difference in the way they perceive or perform that piece. Tell them only that. Put the rest of your impressive research in an e-mail or hand it out. Those who care will have it to read. Those who don't care won't read it, but you won't have wasted your time on them.

Marking scores

Every conductor has his or her own system. There has been a great deal written on the use of colored pencils and what each shade means. I use highlighters to mark my scores, finding that five or six colors are plenty for me. I don't need the 64-color pack. Aubergine and eggplant are the same to me when the music is speeding past my eyes. I may be needing to give the sopranos a dirty look at that point, anyway. By using highlighters, each color has a different meaning and jumps out at you. We all need colorful reminders that the meter is changing or there is a subito piano or fermata or a breath.

TMI can pronounce your rehearsal DOA.

TLC in rehearsal

In order to create a totally satisfying, well-rounded rehearsal, you must have the following ingredients: **A TEAR; A LAUGH; A CHILL BUMP.**

Think about it. What rehearsal experiences have truly moved you and perhaps even changed your life? It is possible that the rehearsal contained just two of the above, but more than likely, it had all three.

Some of our most incredible moments have been in rehearsals, not performances. Allow me to give just one example. We were preparing for the world premiere of our commission, *Sing for the Cure*, with 350 singers, an 80-piece orchestra, soloists, and a narrator. And what a narrator it was: Dr. Maya Angelou. She had not been well herself and her sister had just survived a bout with cancer. We were all ready in the symphony hall awaiting her arrival. As she came on stage we were already thrilled and honored just to be in her presence. Beginning the second narration, about a family member being diagnosed, she began to falter emotionally and at that point simply put her head down on the podium and wept silently as we waited. We will never have a more moving moment. And it happened in rehearsal not in performance.

If <u>you</u> are unable to provide TLC for your chorus, get someone else to do it!

Tear

If you are naturally unexpressive and not open with your emotions, work on it!! Get some therapy. Really!

Laugh

If you are not naturally funny, work on it!!! Learn some jokes. Loosen up.

Chill Bump

If everything in your life is "pretty good," you need to get out a thesaurus and learn some superlatives!!! If you tell your chorus over and over that they are pretty good, they will stop trying.

As stated earlier, the singers are going to mirror you in some very positive and some very scary ways. They are certainly going to mirror your gestures as it pertains to vocal technique. But they are also going to mirror your feelings about the music you have selected (as well as the warm-ups!).

The question, then, is how to engage yourself in the music so that they can mirror your enthusiasm. This absolutely begins in rehearsal. You can't simply work and work week after week with no attention to the "heart" of the music and then at the final rehearsal say, "Oh, yeah, please emote with your faces."

There is a connection that exists between the conductor and the singers in rehearsal that is going to then become the connection mirrored by the audience. Too often we have a disconnect here. As conductors, we get wrapped up in the technicalities of the music and forget that when we do that, so do our singers, and that is what they then reflect to the audience.

The emotional meeting place

There is an emotional "meeting place" that exists between the singers and the audience. It is like reaching your hand out and touching a mirror. There are still two hands, but they are as one. This common ground is where they share the experience completely and equally. However, if the singer steps beyond that line in his/her own experience and becomes too emotional during the singing, the audience automatically pulls back, becomes less involved, and more of a spectator than a participant. This happens, for example, if singers get so emotionally involved that they cry or overly express the music.

On the other hand, if your singers do not involve themselves in the expression of the text and the emotion of the music, the audience notes their lack of engagement and once again will immediately detach from the experience. They will sit back, unmoved, and also become judgmental. The real magic is for the performer and audience to meet exactly halfway and equally share the experience. My personal belief is that your singers will never approach that line with the audience if they are holding folders (except in the case of major works or extended foreign language pieces). The use of music tucks the emotional line, where the chorus might have met the listeners, neatly away in the side pocket of the folder, completely out of reach.

In order for the chorus to find that place, I ask them to practice overstepping the emotional line. For example, if we are singing a song that is emotionally charged, they are asked to focus on someone they have lost, be it friend, relative or even a pet. Then they are directed to fully experience all of the emotions that go with those memories. It doesn't result in very pretty singing, but certainly helps the singers attach an emotional response to their performance and identify the line beyond which they are not to cross later in performance.

When the concert rolls around, they know exactly where that line is because they have already crossed it in rehearsal. At that point, they are able to judge exactly where it is and meet the audience there – every time.

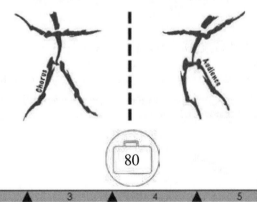

CHAPTER 12

Vocal Health in Rehearsal
Guarding against motion sickness

One of the most important tasks you have when guarding against poor vocal technique in your singers is to listen, listen, listen. That is the obvious part. The other key is to watch them carefully. To my knowledge, no voice teacher or conductor has yet to be sued for malpractice, but I have no doubt that day is coming. Don't be the one who encourages poor vocal health simply by lack of attention!

One of our fine vocal coach neighbors to the north (Toronto, Canada), Donna Flynn, has written a series of fine articles addressing this very thing. One of the articles is titled "Am I Damaging My Voice?" In it she has some wonderful advice.

"While it may be common for your throat to feel strained while singing in groups, such as choirs, it is not normal. This happens when you cannot hear yourself clearly and attempt to be heard by singing over other voices or instruments. You may adjust your singing style in order to blend with the group. To alleviate this, work on your material individually, allowing imbalances that are occurring and unable to be heard by the conductor due to the group environment to be corrected before bad habits form and damage takes place."

"When your throat feels tight or hoarse it is because incorrect vocal cord adjustments occur when moving from one note to the next. Support is lacking, such as breath, to produce sound correctly. Power, fullness and style are attempted by shouting, pushing or forcing the sound into place. The main culprit is a lack of balance between the individual components necessary for singing. These include your mental thoughts while singing, correct posture, breath, tone production, vocal cord adjustments, understanding chest and head registers, resonant sound, and creative expression used to create your distinct style."

What happens when they are actually sick?

What can you do about this? First you can guard against it by educating your singers on the signals of sickness before they get too far along. This is obvious when traveling in the car!

You can do this at the beginning of the year in a communication via e-mail. Most vocal problems result from the following:

1. Short-term upper respiratory illness: cold, flu, sinus, allergies, etc.
2. Gastric issues resulting in reflux
3. Vocal misuse and abuse

The **first** of these is the most prevalent. Your singers need to know when such things are coming on and the difference in the symptoms and remedies. Of course, this is all affected by voice irritants such as pollen, inhaled irritants (pollution), smoke, chemical fumes in addition to the actual illnesses they catch from each other, children, or those pesky door knobs.

The **second**, gastric issues, has become much more prevalent as our diets and eating habits have spun out of control. Your singers absolutely need to know that if they are hoarse for more than 2 weeks in a row, they need to begin to search for the cause. If they rule out respiratory issues, they need to ask their physicians about reflux. This can be chronically burning their vocal folds while they sleep and they don't even know it.

The **third** includes a variety of issues. Most of these are ways in which we encourage misuse of our voices through poor vocal technique in rehearsals and performances. But this can also be a result of lack of education on the basics of vocal health outside of rehearsal as well. We also make demands on our singers, such as oversinging in large halls or over orchestras, changing temperature from space to space, etc.

What can you do to encourage vocal health in rehearsals?

1. Listen, listen, listen. You are the only one actually listening as they sing. Use the entire rehearsal as a laboratory for healthy singing.
2. Encourage your singers to hydrate before coming to rehearsal. It takes at least two hours for your singers to hydrate on the cellular level! It can't be done on the 10-minute drive to rehearsal.
3. Encourage your singers to get plenty of rest in and around rehearsals and performances. There is nothing like a rested body to help provide a rested voice and mind.
4. Encourage your singers to use good posture during rehearsals. Remind them of what that is. Let them sit, let them stand, let them move around.

5. Teach them to breathe. Never let up on this. Remind them often throughout the rehearsal.
6. Remind them not to abuse their voices by speaking (or singing) too loudly. Also encourage them to keep their speaking voice at a normal pitch that is not too low and to conserve their voices, especially on rehearsal and performance days.

Obviously, you are not in a position to prescribe medicine for your singers, but you must at least have a cursory understanding of medications and remedies that are on the market, especially those that are over-the-counter and easily accessible to your singers. Perhaps you have a doctor, nurse, or pharmacist in your chorus who can help with this – or the parent of one of your students. However you get your information, you need to have it.

Of course, we all know that hydration is one of the keys to healthy singing. What you may not know is that it takes about two hours to hydrate from the cellular level. Anything else is topical and does not reach the vocal folds anyway. There is some great information, including a gargle recipe, in *The Perfect Blend* DVD – and a film of my own vocal folds. There is a great deal of information available from many sources, and the information is constantly changing. Since *The Perfect Blend* was published, we have welcomed the arrival of Mucinex on the market and now there is a generic form as well. This is a pill form of guaifenesin that was only available with a prescription until recently. All of these are expectorants that will help make the mucous more fluid, which helps the fleshy covering of the vocal folds remain moist.

Question: What to Do with the Aging Voice?

Answer: Sit-ups.

(Keep reading)

Everywhere I go, I get several recurring questions. One is about the changing voice. I refer them to experts on the subject. Another is about the aging voice. I would be more than happy to refer them to an expert, but since I own an aging voice myself, I should be able to discuss it!

When people ask me what they are to do with that one aging singer whose vibrato has simply widened to a major third, I have a simple answer for them to pass on to those singers. There is a very simple place for them to begin regaining the voice of their golden years: Sit-ups. That usually sends them on their way, seeking other volunteer opportunities.

That may seem harsh. **The answer is not really sit-ups**. But the concept is true. For example, if a gymnast such as Mary Lou Retton decided to jump back on that balance beam, her coach would tell her she needed to start at the beginning to completely retrain her muscles. It wouldn't take her as long as it did the first time, but she would also NEVER reach the heights she once achieved because the muscles simply could never get back to the shape they were in when she was 15! So why do we think the voice is any different?

What to do? The real answer is to maintain good vocal health throughout your life by doing the things you already know. It might not be sit-ups, but it certainly is getting the entire body into as good a shape as possible before assuming that can be done with just the vocal muscle. If your aging singer hasn't done these things, it is never too late to start. Remember, we must start with the big muscle groups to get in shape, not the smallest.

Other advice can include:
Use proper vocal technique in singing and speaking.
Do not smoke.
Hydrate.
Take care of acid reflux and upper respiratory problems.
Be willing to change voice parts as your voice changes and ages.
Embrace a new sound, one with less vibrato and less tension.

Solo singing vs. choral singing

You can just imagine the fine lines I have walked in my careers as private voice teacher, vocal pedagogy teacher, and choral conductor. This has been a lifelong exercise in being politically sensitive.

"Does singing in choir five hours a week hurt my private study and my desire to develop my solo singing career?", they ask.

First, that depends on the choral conductor. Certainly, if he or she subscribes to the sometimes popular stripping away of all individual vocal color and tone in order for the chorus to emit some sound that is foreign to the natural occurrence of people singing together, there is a problem. If they encourage full, healthy singing in the choral setting, it is a different situation altogether.

There is quite a simple answer for vocal students who are seeking solo careers (although not an answer they automatically like to hear). If they are singing five hours in a choir, the simple equation is they have to spend at least five hours a week in serious development of their solo voice to balance those spent in choir.

This is my warning to choral conductors who require their singers to sing straight tone for an hour and a half at a dynamic level of pianissimo. What you are doing would be similar to going to the gym to work out and lifting weights for an hour and a half with only your pinky finger. Then you go away and come back in two days (choir rehearsal) and spend another hour and a half doing the pinky finger exercise again. Over and over. No person in their right mind would do this. The big muscle groups are ignored and eventually will atrophy if not used. You must allow the full use of the vocal muscles for healthy singing and healthy choral technique.

Stress on the voice

According to research done at the Center for Voice Disorder at Wake Forest University in Winston-Salem, NC, singing styles were graded according to laryngeal muscle tension. They were rated on a scale of 1 to 100, 100 being the most tense.
Here are the results:

    96 – gospel singers
    89 – hard rock singers
    86 – country and western singers
    65 – jazz singers
    57 – opera singers
    41 – choral singers!!!

If you ever wanted a case for why people should sing in a choir, here it is. How many times have you heard the studio voice teacher tell a student that singing in a choir will ruin his/her voice? According to the muscle tension scale, that is not the case!

CHAPTER 13

Expect Detours!
Plan your flexibility

Sometimes it doesn't matter how much you plan, there are surprises along the way: road construction that takes longer than you planned; a piece of music you thought was a "slam dunk" ends up being the one that takes five times as much rehearsal and preparation. You have to be ready for these detours and not let it ruin your trip!

Other possible "surprise" detours are:

Pep rallies, other assemblies
Principal interrupting class
Testing days
Costume fittings
Choreography rehearsals
Snow days, hurricanes, floods, locusts
Power outages
Unforeseen occurances in the life of your chorus

The Rehearsal May Not Be a Democracy,
but a Dictatorship Won't Work Either.

Sometimes a trip becomes a democracy (or so they think). There are times when the family gets to vote on what it wants to do next or go next. Most of the time, however, the tour guide (Dad or Mom or whomever) guides those decisions. They don't just say, "We've arrived in New York City, where do you want to eat dinner?" That would be like meeting your chorus and saying, "We are going to give a holiday concert, what do you want to sing?" But allowing them some input increases their investment and their buy-in. But they always need to be guided.

You are going to give your tour group three choices of restaurants, all of which you like and are appropriate in price, cuisine, time allotted to eat, location, etc. Give your singers a choice of three pieces that are all appropriate to the concert, and fit in the overall theme, but allow them to choose. You might even set it up so the result is almost completely predictable and falls the way you wanted it to anyway. "We've arrived in New York City and here are your choices:

1. A brand new fancy French restaurant named "Liver Lovers" that features 20 kinds of pâté.
2. A great new multi-ethnic restaurant named "You Won't Feel Your Tongue for Days" that features the spiciest food on the planet.
3. McDonalds.

You set that one up knowing what they would choose. But they still chose the restaurant and felt some sense of engagement in the process. Don't use this tactic too often, or they will catch on. We do the same thing with music when we allow our choruses to be democracies.

There are times, however, when I have chosen a piece that they simply hate. No longer a democracy, it is a coup d'etat. You may as well toss it quickly. It's not going to get better. In fact, the more you dig your heels in, the more vitriolic their dislike of the piece. It will end in an ugly music-burning party/bonfire after the concert.

The level of collaboration depends on who is traveling with you and the relationship you have with them. You might share the planning or even the driving. When you don't involve others, you must be willing to take all of the blame along with all of the praise. Collaboration is a delicate dance indeed.

Whoever said singers could dance?

While singing opera in Europe, I learned that my bosses simply assumed everyone could do the standard ballroom dances (and fencing, for that matter). There are no lessons, just "Heute üben wir einen Waltz für die Ausstellung morgen abend, *Die Lustige Witwe*." (OK, today we practice the waltz for tomorrow evening's performance of *The Merry Widow*.)

Nothing strikes fear in the heart of a Baptist boy from Texas like being ordered to dance on stage – with a bunch of Europeans – in German, no less! Good thing that my dance partner, Olga, was a hearty Swiss girl accustomed to practicing with a cow. At that moment I longed for the part of the butler who didn't have to dance.

But I found that ballroom dancing is truly an amazing exercise in give and take, alternating between leader and follower. It is one in which every nuance of the partner is utmost. I learned, perhaps for the first time in my life, what it was like to have to follow – especially when given one day to learn to waltz. There is a reason it ultimately works: trust. Your singers "dance" with you for the same reason. They sing for you because they trust you.

What can we learn from stories about dancing?

It takes two to tango. Someone has to lead, but someone else has to follow – willingly! The leader in a dance must be willing to do just what the choral conductor does in a rehearsal. He or she knows where they are headed. The director or dancer knows all of the basic steps, has studied them in one way or another, and even knows some tricks beyond the basic steps. The leader is there not to arbitrarily impose his or her wishes on the other person, but to allow that person the freedom to experience the exercise of dancing with a completely different set of thoughts in mind. Those include being a suitable partner in the process, sometimes helping with decisions, always being prepared at every turn to accept what the leader asks of them.

This partnership is not equal, between dancers, or between conductor and chorus. Imagine two people getting out on the dance floor, the music is playing, others are dancing, and the two people say to each other, "what do you want to do now?" Or imagine the pushing, shoving, and downright ugliness that will ensue if they simply decide who is in charge as they go along. Two pigs in a burlap sack. One thing they will most likely be successful in doing is clearing the floor and providing hours of entertainment for those who have stopped dancing for fear of being trampled.

IS THIS WHAT YOUR REHEARSALS ARE LIKE?
Without a clear plan of what the dance is going to be like, you will waste your time and that of your singers – one of the greatest travesties perpetrated by conductors.

88

On the other end of the spectrum is the dancer who is to lead but does not take into account his partner or her wishes or capabilities. The dancer may decide in advance that his or her favorite dance is the tango and prepare only for this dance. Upon arriving, he meets his partner who aside from being rotund in the extreme, can't move backwards, sideways or even smoothly in the high-top tennis shoes she came in. A long sexy move across the floor ending in a backwards dip is probably not going to happen without a trip to the emergency room for one or the other. What to do? Abandon all hope?

Of course not. This is the parable of the dance captain who did not plan. He is the one who did not take into consideration the capabilities of his partner. This is the conductor who selects repertoire because he likes it, learned it in college or insists on doing it because it will be good for the chorus. They will grow from it, by George. Well, that could have been said by the dance master in the earlier scenario as well. Looking at his dance partner, he could have stuck to his guns and danced the tango until the steps were mastered. But would it ever be a dance. Absolutely not. That only happens in the movies.

This concept was never demonstrated more clearly than in the new hit television series "Dancing with the Stars." Each week, the audience witnesses first-hand the progress made by those who literally give themselves over to their partners and become one unit. It is amazing to watch – as our concerts are amazing to hear when the dance is perfect.

Chapter 14

Maintaining Control
"Mom, he's on my side of the car."

This is a "mini-chapter" on discipline. I know very little about this. Really. My own children were simply perfect (well, almost) and I didn't have to struggle with discipline raising them. I have never taught public schools, so I can't relate to what many of you are going through today. However, there are a few things that I do know and I have found some interesting things from several other authorities.

I watch "Super Nanny" on television all the time. It is like staring at a car wreck – once you look, you just can't turn away. Her method requires a few things that can certainly be tools for us to consider. Some of the things she suggests are:

1. Get down on their level. Now, this is tricky. But what she really means is that you don't want to just tower over them as some tyrannical warlord punishing his subject. I do agree that we can first explain why poor behavior does not help any of us attain our goals. Certainly reasoning with your chorus is not like reasoning with a two-year-old throwing a temper tantrum in the middle of Wal-Mart. Or maybe it is.
2. Make eye contact. This is always important in getting their attention. Once again, you are relating to them human to human.
3. Consistency. You can't be a tyrant one moment and then allow them to run rampant the next.
4. Distract them when they act up. If you keep them busy, they don't have time to act up. This happens most often when you are fumbling for what to do next in rehearsal. If you are following your plan and keeping on task, so will they.

Super Nanny's Last resort: The Naughty Corner!!

Oh, how I would love to have one of those for my adults! But I think they would enjoy it way too much and it would somehow become the most desired place in the rehearsal room.

Remember, you are "called" to be their leader, not their best friend. There is an important part of conducting that requires you to be friendly, open, and even vunerable. But being best friends, by its very nature, requires that you are on the same level. You are not and never will be. You are hired or "called" to be their leader, conductor, teacher, mentor, surrogate parent, pastor, role model, not their best friend.

Kenneth Phillips, in *Directing the Choral Music Program*, describes "Four Modes of Discipline." They are:

1. Authoritarian
2. Neglectful
3. Permissive
4. Authoritative

The **Authoritarian** style requires a high level of control, but whose motivation stems from meeting the needs of the teacher first. The rule is to be obeyed and there are few exceptions. Such teachers are feared.

The **Neglectful** style shows little control in the classroom. It is a typical "don't care" attitude. Little is expected from the students and they expect little from the teacher in return. They use the same old lesson plans and allow students a great deal of freedom in disrupting class.

The **Permissive** teacher loves the kids, they just don't know what to do with them! They fail to see the necessity of boundaries. Anarchy is the rule. This is a danger for beginning students especially. By trying to become their friends, the opposite happens.

The **Authoritative** teacher is assertive but not domineering and is the most successful. The singers are fully engaged in the process. Involvement is high. These teachers understand that a high level of order and control are necessary if education is to take place.

What good does the above information do for us? Well, it at least makes each of us look at our own habits and discipline styles. No doubt we are, once again, combinations of the above, as we were with the types of conductor/teachers. We are also able to identify these traits in our colleagues – both those we admire and those we may only pity! Regardless, it is healthy to do a little inventory of self in order to make appropriate adjustments.

In his book, *Choral Charisma*, Tom Carter gives a new and insightful spin on discipline. He describes creating a safe choral environment where everyone involved is respectful and supportive of one another. In this scenario, the singers will then feel safe. When they feel safe, they allow themselves to be vulnerable and thus connect to each other and the music on a deeper level. This cannot be done in an atmosphere that is filled with judgment, ridicule or teasing. It also cannot be done in a situation that is simply anarchy, when the backseat drivers have been given the steering wheel!

Can we change the way we are? Yes. Is it easy? No.

I have often met people who have lost control of their choir or situation who think moving to a new situation or a new choir or a new city will give them a "new start." Most of the time they find out it was not the choir, the city or the situation, but themselves. They find out they are the same person and the issues have mysteriously "followed" them.

One thing I do know. Once you have "lost it" and yelled at them, you have truly lost it. There is seldom a return from this. They know they got the best of you. And they know what buttons to push to get you back into the out-of-control mode. Never yell at your chorus.

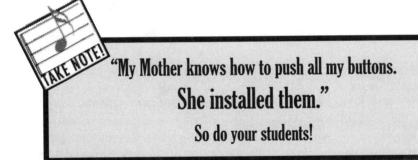

TAKE NOTE!

"My Mother knows how to push all my buttons.
She installed them."
So do your students!

Peer pressure works wonders as well. When my chorus gets too rowdy, the best thing that can happen is for them to self-discipline. You hand them the proverbial paddle and say, "This is not getting us where we want or need to go. I am not the principal or the warden. If someone around you is out of line, ask them to stop."

Chapter 15

What Happens If You Don't Arrive on Time?
The audience will be there regardless.

Adding extra rehearsals at the end is a terrible idea. "No good can come from this," as we say. If you must consistently add rehearsals at the end of the rehearsal period, it is most often 90 percent your fault. This will kill the singers on many levels. They will come to expect it, knowing there will be extra rehearsals thrown in. They will begin to "coast" through the early rehearsals, knowing you will add more at the end, thinking, "What is the point in getting worked up about learning my music when we are going to add rehearsals at the end anyway." In addition, when you add rehearsals at the end in order for them to "cram" for the exam, they will be tired when the performance time arrives. The performance will suffer.

Arriving early is a wonderful thing. Add extra rehearsals at the beginning. What a concept! This gives you the opportunity to sing through the entire concert, in concert order, many times before the performance. It gives you so many other options – such as creative polishing – or, imagine this, canceling a rehearsal or two at the end! It also makes you look brilliant!

Learn from your colleagues in opera, theater, dance, etc.

None of these disciplines would ever enter into a performance situation with as little "dress" rehearsal as we choral conductors do. How many times have you performed a choral concert without ever having sung the entire concert all the way through, in the actual performance space with every "connector" in place, including applause, set changes, etc.

Would this ever happen in opera or theater? Absolutely not. In fact, in most of these situations, there is a tech rehearsal that is a run-through (or maybe a walk-through), a dress tech rehearsal to add even more details (such as costumes, props, lights) and then a dress rehearsal. And in the ideal situation, the night before opening is dark to allow the cast to rest! I don't know anyone who has the luxury of running a rehearsal three nights (or days) in a row and then taking a night off before opening. We would certainly be much better off if we were able to manage this kind of scheduling.

Be flexible

This is not one of the traits most often attributed to conductors (along with humility). But it is certainly one that will make everyone's lives much happier. I told you earlier that every single piece in your repertoire is like a child. Then you were told to be willing to admit that one of the ingredients you chose to put in your concert recipe is not working and be willing to cut it from the program. And I mean be willing to cut it as late as dress rehearsal, even if it is in the printed program. Breathe. Most of your audience is not reading along with you anyway.

By the time you get near performance, every piece on the concert is like your own child. You have selected them, nurtured them, loved them, disciplined them. Can you just exclude a child at the last minute? Well, having two children of my own, I know the answer! The answer is "yes." At the last minute, if you have an unruly child, you sometimes have to exhibit "tough love." That child (piece) has not behaved properly, for whatever reason. In that case, it would be wrong of you to allow that child (piece) to perform. You gain absolutely nothing by digging your heels in and subjecting your audience and your singers to a piece just because you are too stubborn or proud to drop it. Your singers will not trust you the next time this happens!

Dress rehearsal

The day before (or even earlier):
Sing through the entire concert in order – no stops, no starts, as if the audience were sitting right there – and have someone time it. This is just the way they do it in theater, in opera, in musical theater and we in choral music have just gotten away from this tradition. Then, when it is over, you can give "notes" and rehearse whatever didn't go well.

The actual day of the performance:
You do not want to sing all the way through every single piece. It will fatigue your singers' voices, bodies, and minds. You need to do a "cue to cue," meaning you start and stop each piece. You can do the middle of some of the pieces if you need to. If you do this, however, you need to have sung through the entire concert in order, without stops, at the rehearsal prior to "dress."

One of the choral giants of the twentieth century, Lloyd Pfautsch, said the following: "The final rehearsal is the time when the chorus realizes its capabilities and experiences an added or a heightened sense of involvement. If they are ready for this realization and experience, then they have been well prepared during all other rehearsals. If they are not ready, then it is too late for the conductor to recoup the time that has been lost."

It is now too late to do substantive work on the music. There are some things you can actually correct at the last minute that will stick in the performance that will follow minutes later. However, it goes against everything we have discussed about working very hard to move our own time table back – more like the regimen practiced by our colleagues in other performing arts. Often, in the voice studio, we hear, "I will turn on when I get in front of an audience." All too often, we as choral conductors have depended on this same adrenaline rush to kick in and lift our chorus's performance from the mundane to the extraordinary. But gambling is illegal in most states and this is definitely a gamble.

What is the reality of "peaking too soon"? Not when you are working with a group of people and exposing them to new situations and experiences once they get in front of an audience. This is all the more reason to encourage a dress rehearsal that is as close to "performance ready" as possible. Everything should be in place. There should be chill bumps – and even a few laughs and tears.

Imagine, if you will, our colleagues who perform on Broadway. Eight performances a week. How do they keep it fresh and alive? Sure, they are professionals, but it is more than that. It is a combination of extraordinary preparation, a true love of what they are doing, and the final ingredient that happens when the audience arrives. In fact, preparation is not only the key to flawless performances, but is one of the major remedies for stage fright.

Move that rehearsal schedule up!!! Don't worry about "peaking" too soon – better that than peaking the day after the performance.

Chapter 16

The Warm-up Before the Performance
The pep talk/huddle

The day has come. Your singers arrive at least one hour before the performance. You have them for 30 minutes in the hall to warm them up and pump them up. Then the hall opens. You have another 30 minutes backstage, in the gymnasium or the cafetorium. What do you do with these final moments?

During these times, the singers are completely focused on the destination. They know that when they actually arrive, there will be a throng of people awaiting their arrival. The excitement is palpable. The singers have a million things on their minds, including how they look, who is in the audience, and where they are going to eat after the concert.

In the perhaps 30 minutes you have in the hall, you must treat them very gently. This is the time for all musical issues and issues pertaining to the "flow" of the concert. Save all of the other questions or announcements for backstage. Use your 30 minutes wisely. Encourage them.

You have spent weeks working on the finer details of each piece of music. You have taken them apart and hopefully had time to put them all back together. At this point, it is time to give the singers some ideas of what your big picture objectives/visions are. They need some big handles to grab onto at this point. Help them imagine what the emotional roller coaster is going to be like. Help them empathize with what the audience is going to hear and experience. Assign colors or various adjectives to each song to give them an idea of the big picture so everyone is on the same page as to what each song is intended to evoke.

This is definitely the time to start and stop each piece in concert order for several reasons:

1. It reminds them of the order of the pieces.
2. It reminds them of any changes in standing order, sets, etc.
3. It allows you a moment to remind them of the shape and color of each piece.
4. It reminds them you are not going to speak between each song to give them a clue as to what song is next – they already know!

Only musical questions are allowed at this point. Do not allow them to get into the minutiae of costumes, etc. Focus on the music, the sound, the response you are wanting from the audience. Try to make sure all technical issues have already been dealt with before this.

Let them leave the stage, do what they need to do, then meet somewhere about 15 minutes before curtain.

The pep talk/huddle

Save your best shot for the final words of the pep talk. This is the "huddle" before taking the field. It is where you are transformed from coach to cheerleader! Once again, if you are uncomfortable doing the "touchy feely," then you must get someone else to do it – do not simply leave it out because it is not in your personality profile to do such things.

Mirrors!

1. First, check yourself in the mirror to make sure there are no wardrobe malfunctions. Take a hard look at your face and what you are telegraphing!
2. The singers are going to mirror you – your attitude, your stress level, your comfort level, your ease at making music, your pride in them.
3. The audience is going to mirror the singers as they mirror you!
4. Have the singers check each others' attire.

Allow the singers to speak at this point. Direct the comments so you don't get, "Hey, Dr. Seelig, remember the time in rehearsal when we had that food fight? That was awesome." That can kill the mood. Ask questions about what this concert means to them or if they have special guests in the audience they would like to tell us about. It is amazing what these little moments do to unify the group and give them an even deeper sense of investment.

This is a good time to remind them of why you are all there, why you have gone to the trouble to work this hard, to take this journey together. This is the time to focus on the big picture and even visualize what it is going to be like when the last note is sung. Touching each other is a good thing. Feeling the unity and energy and bringing the weeks and weeks of hard work to a culmination is an important exercise.

Part Three
The Trip Home: Post-concert

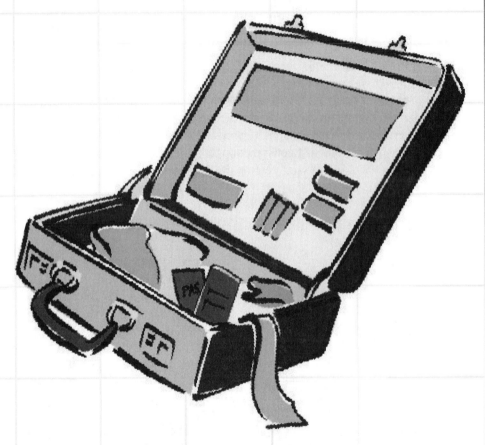

Saying "Thank you" with Grace

Evaluating the Trip

Evaluating the Tour Guide

Chapter 17

Saying "Thank You" with Grace

First things first. One of the most important lessons you must learn and that you must teach your students is to be gracious in accepting praise immediately following the performance. (Thanks, Mom, for this one!) Here is the scenario. Concert is over. There is a line of people wanting to congratulate you (or your singers).

Fan: That was the most beautiful concert I have ever heard.

Singer: Really? Thanks, but we have sung better.

Fan: I can't imagine how it could possibly have ever sounded better.

Singer: You should have heard us in dress rehearsal or at last night's performance – it was so much better!

Fan: (trying one more time) Well, that is great, but I cried all the way through the second half; you all sang so beautifully.

Singer: That's nice. But we really weren't that together in our interpretation and the vowel colors all seemed to go awry, the cutoffs were just sloppy, sloppy, and I had indigestion. And those sopranos!

Fan: (near tears again) Well, I'm sorry I missed you at your best.

The singer just told the fan that they were stupid, had no taste, and a tin ear.

The lesson: Just say "Thank you very much."

Be gracious and take the praise when you can get it!!! You'll have time to pick the concert apart when you are alone or alone with your singers.

Chapter 18

Evaluating the Trip and the Tour Guide
Did you purchase the video?

How does the evaluation affect rehearsal technique and what can be different in rehearsals that could have changed the product.

There are three stages to the memories of any trip:

Immediate
Medium
Long-term

Immediate: These are the first things you think when the experience is fresh. "On our trip to Paris last week, the lines were so long we couldn't get up the Eiffel Tower. The food was horrible. They only put one ice cube in my coke. The cab drivers were rude The air conditioning didn't function like at home. We were really tired by the time we got to see the Mona Lisa and not only was she not smiling very much, but she was really small and we couldn't even get close because of all the people holding their hands up taking pictures of her with their cell phones. It was just crazy. There were too many tourists!"

These include such things as "We sang flat, we missed an entrance, we blatted the high notes, we forgot part of one piece, the altos were completely off in one part, the concert lasted three hours, etc."

Medium: These remain for some weeks. You share these with people who ask about your trip but don't need to know the gory details: "Paris was so beautiful. The Louvre was every bit as fabulous as it appeared in *The da Vinci Code*. The Eiffel Tower is simply amazing – you can see it from everywhere in the entire city. The ham and cheese crepe I ate on the street next to Notre Dame was the best Hot Pocket I ever had."

These include such things as "The concert was wonderful. It had a few minor flaws here and there, but overall it was a beautiful evening. We might have done better on a few things, but overall it was lovely."

Long-term: These are the memories we will share when rocking on the porch someday. "Paris is the most romantic city in the world. Everything about it is completely magical. There is not one thing I would change about my trip. I remember the food, the wine, the people, everything as being simply perfect."

"The concert was simply life-changing – for the singers and audience. We were as close to perfection as any chorus has ever been. There were moments of such sheer beauty, the audience absolutely held their breath."

Aside: I have described concerts as "breathtaking" before and it wasn't all that nice!

In days gone by, when we didn't record every single note and every single move we made on DVD, CD, mini-disc or cell phone, we could get away with the long-term memories much easier. Not so much anymore. There are definitely some performances left better to memory than Memorex!

This is one point at which you must become a master. How much do you share with your singers? How can you be objective about the performance but still be encouraging and make them want to go out and do it again. How do you find that fine line between the parents who began weeping merely at the sight of their son or daughter in a formal gown or tux and to whom every note was angelic and the reality displayed graphically on the DVD?

Sharing the memories

What souvenirs are you going to bring home from this trip?

> A post card or poster advertising the concert
> A program
> A ticket stub
> CD of the performance
> DVD of the performance
> Photos of the performance
> Memories from singers and audience members

Kudos

One of the things we do a terrible job of as conductors is passing on compliments to the chorus. We take all the bows, hear the great things people say, and forget to pass them on. Encourage your singers to process their experience – both verbally and in writing. This can take place during a brief time following each performance when you allow the singers to share comments of friends and family. But they can also write them down.

And it is not just following a concert that people send comments.
The e-notes take care of this. We add letters, comments, entries on our Website guest book to the e-notes that are sent to the singing members each week. This does not cost us a penny and it does wonders for the members to actually share the compliments. Now, members will e-mail comments they hear so that we can include them in the notes. We can never boost our chorus morale enough. The words of others go a long, long way to motivating them to keep working harder.

Evaluating the Tour Guide

Did you guide exactly as you had hoped?

If you are planning to share the CD or the DVD with the chorus, you need to watch it first! That way you know what you need to say to them. You can't always blame it on the sound guy or the video guy or the lighting guy. And hopefully the camera did not spend too much time on you (unless it was one of your family members doing the taping).

In looking back, have you done some of the following big "no-no's"?

The Conductor Who Won't Shut Up
The Conductor Who Steals the Show
The Conductor Who Hogs the Bows

The Conductor Who Won't Shut Up

Most people in the audience want to hear the conductor talk at some point. If you don't say a word, or if no one says a word, there is a disconnect; the performers don't seem like real people. I have heard incredible choral concerts where no one said a single word. Why not just purchase the recording? And they don't want to hear you read, either. They assume that if you are smart enough to become the conductor of a chorus, you can read! They want to hear you talk to them!

However, no one (not even Mom) wants to hear the conductor talk between every song or piece. I repeat, no one. Well, except maybe the conductor's Mom. And the worst phrase a conductor can possibly utter is "This next song is about…." **Just say "no." Don't ever do it.**

There is nothing more amateurish (in the bad sense), or condescending for that matter, than to remind the audience after every song what is about to happen: **another song**! They know that. They have a program, for heaven's sake. The only possible response to that is "Duh!" You have spent hours being creative with the music on your program. Spend at least that much time being creative about what you, or someone else, is going to say.

Planning is the key. Few are able to simply "wing it." And don't read it, either. You are going to memorize your music, you or the narrator can memorize the spoken words as well. If you are uncomfortable speaking, then choose someone from your chorus to "narrate." Save the history and analysis for the program notes! This is not the time to read from Groves or Grout. Lastly, try not to open a concert with talking or announcements or a welcome from some person in your organization. The audience came to hear music. At least let them start by hearing music. Save the talking for after the first piece or just before intermission, if there is one.

The conductor who steals the show

It is always good from time to time to have someone videotape just you during a performance. This is completely humbling. If you have seen either of the PBS documentaries on the TCC, you know they had one camera isolated and pointed at me, back toward the audience. Ouch! I was horrified, of course. I didn't remember making all those faces.

I have also had myself videotaped from behind during a concert to learn the following things: what the audience was seeing from behind; if my gestures were a help or a distraction to the singers; was I in any way hindering the audience from focusing on the music or the ensemble. This is a very important lesson for all of us to learn. Not an easy one, but important nonetheless. If I grandstand and pull focus from the music and the singers, it should be my choice to do so.

In the case of conducting a chorus, smaller is better. I learned from a band director that if the group is not watching or not following, the answer is to make the beat pattern SMALLER, not LARGER. The less they watch, the bigger we ordinarily make our beat pattern, assuming that they just can't see us! It works. The only time I really want anyone behind me to see my gestures is if I choose to let them, just for effect. Other than that, I am conducting for the chorus, not for the audience! Leave that to the orchestra conductors.

Negate

If you are not familiar with this term, it means to make your beat pattern only large enough for those who need to see it or stop conducting altogether if no one needs you! You don't have to beat every beat of every measure from the first note to the last. You only have to conduct when someone needs you – which is less often than you might think. I know it hurts, but it happens, so deal with it. If you have a competent accompanist, it is insulting for you to turn to them with a huge preparatory beat and, facing them so the audience can see your every move, conduct them through the entire introduction. If you are unable to stop conducting completely at times because of some long-held belief that the world will stop if you do, then at least NEGATE, meaning make the beat pattern as small as humanly possible and still communicate all of the necessary instructions to your chorus.

The conductor who hogs the bows

Let your chorus bow. You didn't get here by doing all the work yourself. But they absolutely do not need to bow, nor do you, after every piece. This will wear everyone out and ruin the flow of your concert.

There is a detailed and fun demonstration of exactly how to bow in *The Perfect Blend* DVD. You can divide the concert (ahead of time and in your performance plan) to include the following:
1. Segues between pieces (no bows – most of the pieces)
2. Bows for you (use sparingly)
3. Bows for soloists or featured groups
4. Bows for the full chorus
Upon your signal to the chorus, they bow counting to four as they bend at the waist and to four as they stand back up. This will provide a uniform, professional look. They can count out loud, because the audience will be applauding. You should never signal for them to do a full chorus bow if the audience is silent!

Part Four: Souvenirs
The kitchen sing(k)

BONUS – Rehearsal Technique by Dr. Jo-Michael Scheibe

To memorize or not to memorize

The perfect blend

Not your '50s family vacation

Some simple do's and don'ts

Rehearsal plan

Musical mishaps

What others say about rehearsals: conductors, singers, and visitors

Chapter 19 ... BONUS!!

Rehearsal Technique
Dr. Jo-Michael Scheibe

One of the preeminent conductor/teachers of our day is Jo-Michael Scheibe, Director of Choral Studies, Frost School of Music, University of Miami. Recently, I was lucky enough to attend a conducting workshop he was giving. His topic was "Rehearsal Technique." I couldn't believe it. I thought, "This is fantastic, I can borrow (steal) some of the information. He had been speaking for only 10 minutes when I realized the information was just too good to "steal." He agreed to share it for this chapter.

Jo-Michael's perspective, while including all types of varied choral experiences, comes more from the university setting where mine is more influenced by the community chorus experience. There is so much wonderful information here, I encouraged him to leave it in the format in which he presented it because the information is easily accessible and understandable. I am very indebted to him for sharing this with me – and with you.

Effective Rehearsal Leadership
Time management in the choral rehearsal.

Leadership is social influence on mission accomplishment. It is getting effective cooperation of other people to harness the resources provided by that cooperation toward the attainment of a particular goal.

Conduct comes from the Latin word *conducere,* which means to lead together. In English, it means to direct the course or guide or lead.

So how do we lead and guide?
I believe it is all about goal-setting.

Goal-Setting:

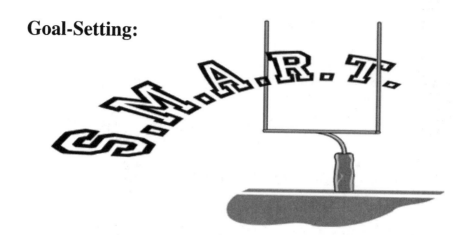

Specific, Measurable, Accountable, Realistic, and Timed.

Specific.   Share these with the choir. Define the result you wish to achieve so there will be no doubt when it has been accomplished or achieved. Avoid using terms like "more," "better," "lots," etc. Give them specifics.

Measurable. There should be quantitative results. Define results that can be measured by someone not involved in the process or the program.

Accountable. Share the goal with someone or some group to which you are answerable.

Realistic. Make sure that the results are indeed attainable so that all involved can believe in success. The goal should also be challenging enough to encourage growth.

Timed. There needs to be a specific date to reach the expected results, allowing sufficient time for the full realization of results: memorization, concert, convention, etc.

So how do we become SMART(er) in our choral rehearsals?

Let's look at successful rehearsals.

We all agree that:

1. Rehearsals are fundamental in building great choirs.
2. Score preparation is crucial.
3. Appropriate music selection by the conductor is paramount.
4. Rehearsals should be stimulating, exciting, and creative.

All of these qualities are necessary for the conductor to build a quality organization. And it is about <u>organization</u>!

For years, I have kept coming back to the question as to why some rehearsals are more successful than others. Fundamentally, as a younger teacher, I believed that it had to do with the students, the weather, their personal relationships with parents, friends, boy or girlfriends. Then Rod Eichenberger started talking about the Golden Proportion. As I left USC and started experimenting with choral rehearsals, I began to do more reading on this concept of Golden Proportion. This is also called the Fibonacci sequence. Many of you may have come in contact with this in various places in your studies. It was even present in the recent book and movie, *The da Vinci Code*.

So what is this sequence and what does it have to do with our rehearsals?

Leonardo Fibonacci was born in the twelfth century and studied sequential numbers. He came up with the sequence 0:1:1:2:3:5:8:13:21:34, etc. (you can say the smaller is to the larger as the larger is to the sum of the prior two). He also discovered that the Golden Mean occurs at approximately 61.8 percent, roughly meaning that the point of most interest or of golden proportion is at that point.

This sequence can be applied to all good art, architecture, music, sea shells, mathematics, etc. There exists a concept that when items are truly in proportion, one will find the Golden Mean at 61.8 percent. This can be seen in structures such as the Parthenon, Leonardo's art, Michelangelo's David, the Stradivarius violin, Beethoven's Fifth Symphony, etc.

Both of these principles, the Golden Proportion and the Fibonacci sequence, can be used to motivate our singers and build a more successful model for our choruses. If we build our rehearsal, keeping in mind this Golden

Proportion and Motivational Growth curve, in a traditional 60-minute rehearsal it might look something like this:

- Warm-ups 1:2:3: (6 Minutes).
- First piece (5 minutes), building on the basics of your warm-ups. Work section with lower tessitura.
- Second piece (8 minutes), fixing small problem spots quickly.
- Third piece (13 minutes), more complicated work.
- Fourth composition (21 minutes) – Golden Mean – this is where the bulk of your work needs to be, the most intense work.
- Conclude with a final selection or two, giving them with a sense of success. Leave them singing as rehearsal ends.
- Tell them they did a good job.

Each successful rehearsal will have the following attributes:

- Direction.
- Defined duration.
- Maximum intensity at the appropriate time.
- The feeling of success.
- A work in progress.
- Stated expectations or goals.
- Use of gesture rather than speech whenever possible to solve musical problems.
- Start and end on time.
- Music listed on the blackboard – more music than is possible   to get through.
- Clean, orderly, bright rehearsal room.
- Order and organization demonstrated by the conductor.
- Singers share in the responsibility of the rehearsal.
- Singers are engaged through questions.
- Set a level they must work to attain.
- Keep the body free from tension.
- Every minute counts in the rehearsal.
- Live with errors in the beginning to show confidence in their abilities as singers and maintain spontaneity.

Maintaining energy and interest in rehearsal

- Use humor.
- Respect your singers.
- Be enthusiastic.
- Score preparation - Do it!
- Value choristers time by being prepared.
- Warm rehearsal demeanor.
- High attainable goals.

To build further success as a conductor you should:

- Have empathy with your singers.
- Try to solve problems with gestures rather than words.
- Plan those rehearsals!
- Make sure everyone has their own folder. They will know that they are part of a bigger organization. They will take ownership of "my music." It will give them a desire to learn. It also signals that "We're going to work!"
- Have a significant amount of music in their folder that is unfamiliar (sometimes groups revert to bad habits on songs they have sung before).
- Hold the rehearsal in a location other than where they perform.
- Build your rehearsal plan on the "Solo Recital format," starting with vocally easy music at the beginning of the rehearsal, the most difficult in the middle, and easing off at the end.

Motivation is the most important part of learning. How we act as conductors will result in what we get from our students.

- We succeed through success.
- To continue to succeed there has to be a new goal after we have finished one success.
- We have to manipulate points of successes by pointing our successes that might have gone unnoticed.
- A teacher must accept his humanity and deal with it in an adult way. He must accept his and his students' fallibility.
- Send "we" rather than "you" or me messages.
- Use positive first – resort only to negative as a last resort.
- Do not talk down to your choir.

Twelve Roadblocks to Mutual Learning:

1. Ordering, commanding, directing.
2. Warning and threatening.
3. Moralizing or preaching.
4. Advising or offering solutions.
5. Giving logical arguments.
6. Indulging, criticizing, disagreeing.
7. Name-calling.
8. Praise agreeing (i.e., phony praise).
9. Reasoning or sympathizing.
10. Interrogating.
11. Withdrawing.
12. Sarcasm.

AND remember there are currently some 15 million singers in the U.S. Ninety-five percent of them do not study voice, and it is our responsibility to teach them healthy vocal habits in the choral rehearsal.

Chapter 20

To Memorize or Not to Memorize?
That is not a question.

You know, there is just not enough time to debate this here. And since this book is not a debate, but one person's opinion, here you go.

The reasons to memorize are completely compelling. If we could simply listen to two choirs back to back singing the same repertoire, one with music, the other without, the answer would most likely be clear. Most of the reasons not to memorize are not as clear.

Bottom line is, with the exception of major works, not memorizing is only laziness. There is no debate about the communication level of using music or not using music. This includes communication between you and your singers, and between your singers and the audience that took the trouble to come hear them perform. Music sets up a barrier between performer and audience. It tends to make the experience an objective one for the audience rather than a shared, subjective one. In many regards, using music squelches your own possibilities of music-making. Just because you rehearsed a certain way doesn't mean you are going to feel it is best in the performance. Be flexible with that. Allowing your singers to use music as a crutch only removes all possibility of spontaneity and making music in the moment. If you suddenly try to make a change because it feels right at the moment, some of your singers will not be looking up and there ensues a mighty train wreck. We've all heard them.

Some years back, I was asked to be the interim choral conductor at a university. I was thrilled. I went into the task with great excitement, expecting to do a wonderful job. In all honesty, it turned out to be less than wonderful.

First, I told the college students that we were going to memorize everything that was not a major work. In the two years I conducted the choruses, the only thing we did not memorize completely was *Carmina Burana* (and I really wanted to memorize that).

The most shocking thing was the resistance I experienced when I told them they would not be needing their 30-pound black folders during performances because it was all going to be in their heads. The initial response was "We don't memorize here." I then asked the simple question, "How many of you memorized your music in high school?", to which I received a 100 percent affirmative answer. The next question was also a simple one. "Then what in the world did you do during the summer between high school and college that allowed you to lose so many brain cells that you can no longer achieve something that came so naturally before summer break?"

We began to memorize.

The next challenge was from faculty members who felt the students were having to memorize too much music. After all, they had to memorize music for juries, recitals, opera scenes, etc. Singing in choir is no less important than any of the other educational experiences they are having in college. In my mind, it may be even more important.

We continued to memorize.

For most of the people in our choirs, they will spend the rest of their lives as either members of or conductors of some kind of choir. Few will spend the rest of their lives on the operatic stage or the recital circuit. The preparation, training, and experiences we provide them in choir are going to prove to be much more practical and indeed long-lasting than those they receive some other places. In my opinion, we need to focus on the priority of educating our singers through the choral experience.

One of my greatest memories was memorizing Ralph Vaughn Williams's *Dona Nobis Pacem*. The performance was one I shall never forget. The students not only sang it beautifully, but completely from the heart and directly to the hearts and minds of the audience – nothing in between.

TAKE NOTE!

**If our goal is communication,
If our goal is to change our audience,
If our goal is to meet them at the emotional line,
If our goal is to use music as a means, not an end,
Then we simply must memorize!**

Memory Tips

1. Sing every song every week. This means you may work on the details of several different songs throughout rehearsal, but you may not leave out any songs for over a week. If you only have one rehearsal a week, this is difficult, but it can be done.

2. Give pop tests. Just when they least expect it, have them put their music down. They will surprise themselves (and you) at how much they remember.

3. Memorize the ends of pieces first. The singers will look forward to knowing the end of each piece best instead of least.

4. Cheat sheets. Pass out sheets with all of the texts written as poetry (which, of course, it all is). This is a great way to wean your chorus, and also a way to familiarize them with the text itself.

5. Hand out a memory schedule in advance. Let them know what is expected and when. You can't memorize an entire concert and expect that the first time they will sing it from memory is dress rehearsal. My suggestion is a schedule that includes one easy piece and one difficult piece per week, leading up to the entire concert memorized at least two weeks before the performance.
Bragging rights: my chorus memorizes a two-hour concert approximately every eight to ten weeks, and they are all volunteers.

6. If you are frightened about going cold turkey on the memorization, try it for half of a concert. Let the chorus use music for the other half, or share the concert with another interesting ensemble, choral or not.

7. Always begin by being firm, and convince the singers you are serious about no books. If you have the slightest lack of confidence, they will see it in your eyes and hear it in your voice and they know you will cave in at the end.

8. Rehearsal CDs. There is as much debate about this as there is memorization. The pros and cons could fill a separate book. Use your own judgment on this.

Suggestion:

At least attempt a concert (or portion) from memory. Make a list of attainable memorization dates. Make cheat sheets of all of the texts. Plan your rehearsal well in advance so you can hit every song every week.

You and your audience will have a more satisfying experience if you allow your choir to sing a 45-minute set from memory and fill out the program with small groups, soloists, duets, and guests rather than sing 90 minutes holding music and boring everyone to tears.

I recently did a workshop at Stetson University with their top choir being the guinea pigs. It was early in the fall semester. I asked their conductor, Alan Raines, to have them sing something for me. They did not reach for music. It never crossed their minds. And boy, did they sing. Exquisitely. When I recovered enough from the beauty of the singing, I continued with the workshop. There wasn't much to say; my faith was renewed in the brain power of university choirs. Thanks, Alan.

Chapter 21

The Perfect Blend
Blend doesn't have to be bland

How many times have you said to your chorus: "I want you to sound like one voice." But you never tell them which one. We just never think to tell them that! So, everyone assumes it is them.

In my experience, it has been beneficial to find a voice in each section that you find most fits the color and style of the piece you are working on. This will not be the same singer for every piece.

Ask that singer to sing a phrase for the chorus. Then, add singers to that voice, encouraging them to listen as they join in so they do not radically change the combined sound and color of the original singer. If you do this in each section, you will then only have the task of combining the sections to come up with the "one voice" you were looking for. This is similar to the voice-matching, assigned-seating exercise that is so helpful in placing voices that complement each other.

If, for some reason, your chorus does not produce a "blended" sound, the conductor has to be able to find out what is wrong. Perhaps the color is wrong, perhaps the vowel is wrong, perhaps the pitch is wrong. Blend is not the result of one thing or the other, but the combination of many things.

BLEND BEGINS FROM THE BOTTOM UP
(not imposed from the top down).
BLEND happens in the following order:
Posture
Breathing
Phonation
Resonance
Vowels

This is much like the parable of the car that stops on the freeway. The driver checks everything from the "carbinator" to the windshield wiper fluid, to no avail. He was out of gas! We choral directors start at the wrong end of the list trying to achieve blend. We work and work on "placement," on matching vowels, on ripping all individual vocal color from every voice to try to achieve the elusive blend.

Where we need to begin is with POSTURE! Make sure your chorus understands how the entire body works in concert with the vocal apparatus. The next step toward achieving blend is BREATHING. If half of your chorus is heaving their chests in clavicular breathing and the other half are using caved-in chests and abdominal breathing, you will never get the result you desire.

After posture and breathing are working well, one of the most important concepts that all of your singers must agree on is BREATH PACING and freedom of the actual vocal folds. If half of your singers are singing with tight, hyperfunctional phonation and the other half are at the other end of the spectrum (pendulum) with hypofunctional, breathy phonation, it doesn't matter what kind of work you do on vowels or tone color. It will never happen for you.

Only after your singers have agreed on these three steps, will you be able to move to the "icing" on the cake: resonance, vowel shape, color, articulation, etc. The combination of all of these will result in that elusive concept known as "blend."

At that point, the singers need to know what shapes you want. At the very least, they need to look like they are all singing the same vowel. I am sure you have probably seen photos of your chorus while singing. From the shapes of the mouths (and facial expressions) of your singers, they could be singing completely different songs.

Blend is also about balance of the resonance each of the singers is providing. If you have an operatically trained singer on one end of the spectrum with "ring for days" and a complete novice with a breathy, unpleasant sound on the other end, your challenge is to bring the two together.

Your own theory on blend also depends on the aural modeling that you, as a conductor and singer, have adopted. If you go back and listen to the recordings you selected as your favorite – your Top 5 – it may give you an indication of what you are looking for in your own choir.

My own theory is this: when working with amateur singers (not students preparing for operatic careers), probably 80 percent of those singers can sing successfully in my chorus and use 100 percent of the individuality inherent in their voice. There may be 10 percent who need to only use 90 percent of the color and timbre they possess. The final 10 percent (if we are lucky enough to have such singers who really want to be a part of a choir) will have to adjust accordingly to the group. I don't think I have ever asked a singer to remove more than perhaps 25 percent of their individual vocal prowess. And I am sure that was a first tenor.

There are conductors who want all of the singers to remove all of the individual color of their voices in order to achieve a unified sound. Surely those conductors are not still reading this book.

So, when people ask me "What is blend?" and I say, "It begins with posture," I get the same blank stares as when asked about the aging voice for which my answer is "sit-ups." It is certainly not what most people expect, but it is, in my opinion, the answer.

Chapter 22

Not your '50s Family Vacation

Times have certainly changed. Those of who are a little older remember what studying music was like before cassette recorders, Xerox machines, CD players, digital voice recorders, IPods, etc. I know this is going to be very foreign to many of you, but we used to actually have to purchase every piece of music we sang – in choir or in our private lessons. Nor did we record every note we ever sang. Thanks to that lack of recorded evidence, those were obviously the golden days and we delivered some flawless performances (legends in our own minds).

What prompted this nostalgic look back? While doing research for this book, I came across a true gem in a half-price book store. The title was *The Art of Conducting*. Written by Michael Bowles with an introduction by Sir Adrian Boult, the jacket copy described it as "A book for the music lover and student of conducting – orchestra, band, choir or glee club." I snatched it up. The book stated boldly, "For every beginning conductor." There was even an entire chapter titled "Rehearsal." This would provide the perfect "historical" perspective of rehearsal technique of 50 years ago. I began to read.

Obvious waste of time and effort undermines all discipline. In any situation the respect of the players for the conductor and his real control over them depend absolutely on whether his demands are seen to be adequate on the one hand and reasonable on the other. Too much rehearsal may easily spoil the freshness and excitement of a performance, just as too little may spoil security in technical detail. When we are thinking about the amount of rehearsal adequate to the achievement of an artistic purpose, we ought to keep in mind at the same time that good music is robust. While everyone concerned would aim at perfection, we must distinguish between perfection and that perfection-ism which can be something of a vice. This communication of excitement is the first attribute of a successful concert and should be the principal aim of a conductor.

Everything not directly related to the work in hand (administration, questions, etc.) ought to be excluded from the rehearsal period. It is also wise for the conductor never to approach the podium until everything is ready for him to begin. This seems a pretty obvious point. It is also wise to leave the podium and the rehearsal room immediately after the rehearsal is over and to attend elsewhere to any matters arising. The value of this is that it tends to condition the players to associate a conductor's presence on the podium with a concentration on rehearsal work and nothing else.

Oh, to be a conductor in the '50s! Then the real fun began!!!

It has not been entirely unknown for a player, especially in the back of the orchestra, to light a cigarette during rehearsal or have a quick look at the day's newspaper when he sees on his part rest marks to the value of a hundred measures or so. Obviously a practice of this kind should be discouraged. Behavior of this kind is no contribution to the general atmosphere of concentration.

Not to mention the lungs of the wind players and everyone else! If smoking in rehearsal wasn't fun enough, he moved on to choral singing.

Happily, a consideration of the detail of voice-training is not too important in the rehearsal of a chorus. The conductor is more concerned with the blend of the voices than the training of the individual. Most composers of choral works have had in mind the normal choral society composed of amateur singers, and the musical effects which they may hope for can be achieved with a group of singers whose voices taken one by one might not be very interesting. Assuming that the part-writing is good, the basis of good choral singing lies simply in having all the singers know all the notes. Singing pleasantly and well requires much less technical training than playing on any instrument with equal satisfaction. Uncertainty in three or four singers at a critical point can spread unreasoningly and unexpectedly through a whole group, just as panic may suddenly arise in a combat group in battle. In choral work, therefore, the first and most important matter to be attended to is a completely thorough drill in the notation.

After reading that book, I had to have a cigarette myself, just to calm down. No wonder orchestral conductors and instrumentalists don't consider singers as musicians!

Chapter 23

What Others Have to Say About the Trip
Conductors, singers, and visitors

In writing a book on a topic such as this, one realizes that your personal experience colors every area discussed. Certainly we have all participated in many rehearsals in our lives other than those we conducted. But we have viewed all of them through our own filters of what we think works best and is most productive. So, it became important to invite conductors, singers, and non-singers from around the country to add their comments about what makes a "perfect rehearsal." I am so grateful to all of the following colleagues who have contributed their thoughts. The overriding response was, "There is no such thing as a perfect rehearsal." And I had to agree. But if there were such a thing, these are the things that would make them that way.

Conductors

Vance George
Conductor: San Francisco Symphony Chorus, 23 years
Winner of 4 Grammy awards

Perhaps my best rehearsal was my last rehearsal with my San Francisco Symphony Chorus. We had already had five rehearsals on Verdi's *Requiem.* It was to be our last rehearsal before Maestro James Conlon arrived to conduct six performances. I walked in ready to just listen and address what needed tidying up or even outright rehearsed. There was a lightness about the whole evening which was the result of knowing the piece, where to pour on the sound and where to articulate and where to exaggerate. I just kind of sat there in my conductor's chair and took stock, stopped when necessary, and made comments. We sang more and I joked with the singers. Basically, we had fun. We knew there would be six performances to polish and we did that. But it was confidence that made it fun. Conductors, know your music! Give markings or add markings that will make the next rehearsal more successful and make sure absentees get those added markings.

Worst rehearsal? Well, that is easy. The piece was 12-tone. We were slugging our way through it and we all hated the music. I'm glad we are over

121

that particular period of musical structure. My dissertation was on 12-tone procedure, so I'm aware of good and bad 12-tone. It was a commission so we had no choice!

Philip Brunelle
Artistic Director, Founder
VocalEssence, Minneapolis

If music is the path you want to pursue, it is important to know that you are the servant. You are there to serve – to help others understand what it is that makes music so meaningful to you. You must be prepared and be ready to lead others toward the musical goal, of course, and you must believe in yourself as a vessel, a voice. On a daily basis – in rehearsal after rehearsal – this is the path, and the rewards are overwhelming!

Dennis Coleman
Artistic Director, Seattle Men's Chorus
Artistic Director, Seattle Women's Chorus

I know it's been the perfect rehearsal when singers leave with more energy – mental and spiritual – than when they arrived. If I've paced the rehearsal correctly, the final 10 minutes aren't spent watching the clock. The singers are involved physically and mentally and leave the rehearsal humming the final tune. This doesn't happen by chance. Every minute of the rehearsal period is planned in advance to engage the mind and body.

Dr. Sandra Snow
Conductor, Michigan State University Women's Chamber Ensemble
Michigan State University School of Music

I have writer's block about this, oddly enough. Since I've never experienced a perfect rehearsal, it is hard to be witty and smart about something I don't often experience! Rehearsals feel messy, chaotic, sometimes full of expressive moments, sometimes not. The perfect rehearsal? I don't get perfect rehearsals any more than I get perfect performances. Perfect rehearsals must belong to other conductors. Perfect conductors.

Conductors who can predict, with certainty, every sound they will hear, anticipate every adjustment they must make, choose music that in every bar and every measure is suited to their particular ensemble. Conductors that have all the answers and are unafraid, in fact obliged, to pour them into their ensemble members. Conductors that are exquisitely prepared, and have hours and hours of score study built into their perfect days. Conductors that wear perfect concert clothes that never bulge, tear, indiscreetly display, or otherwise distract.

I think I'll stick with my messy, chaotic, surprising, estrogen-dominated rehearsals. We have fun.

Dr. James Jordan
Associate Professor
Westminster Choir College

I have always believed that a great rehearsal resides in two distinct areas. (1) How do we make a choir musically "willful" and (2) How much responsibility can I heap upon the choir in a positive way, so they bear the responsibility for the actual music making. I also believe that a vibrant rehearsal has frequent moments of quiet and calm so that great sounds can grow out of them.

Dr. Jonathan Reed
Associate Professor of Music
Michigan State University

The perfect rehearsal for me is almost an "out of body" experience. It is quickly paced. I am never at a loss for creative solutions to problems, and all of my suggestions work instantly. The singers are energized, enthusiastic, and eager. It is a time for laughter, joy, exuberance, and can also be a time for pathos and grief; it depends on the literature being rehearsed. It is, in a word, "sensual." It is also when I don't have to supply all of the answers – I merely ask the questions and the singers do the rest! In that regard, they take ownership of the interpretation.

Incredible rehearsals are almost always the result of very, very detailed score study. There is no substitute for knowledge of score and it is that in-depth knowledge that is incredibly freeing in the rehearsal process. It makes the ears better and it enables one to be almost improvisatory in reaction to the sounding.

Dr. William Powell
Associate Professor of Music
Assistant Director of Choral Activities
Auburn University

As a conductor, my students express more excitement about my rehearsals wherein 1) they become more engaged with the meaning of the text; 2) the pacing of the rehearsal moves briskly; 3) they are challenged to listen, analyze, and "fix" their musical or vocal problems; 4) within a single rehearsal, they sing a variety of repertoire encompassing a noticeable range of style periods, moods, tempi, dynamics, tonalities, etc. Also, I find that they seem more motivated when I demand more from them than what they probably think they can produce during a single rehearsal.

Dr. John Paul Johnson
Director of Graduate Studies and Choral Activities
The University of Kansas

Best rehearsal:
When I had the good fortune to study conducting with Robert Fountain, he often shared a line that is as true today as it has been for decades. This is that there are no bad choirs; only bad choir directors.

I have to prepare as though each rehearsal will be the best. Will I be able to share my knowledge of the music through my preparation, gestures, instruction, and continual evaluation of what my choir is offering? Will I be able to encourage and inspire? Will I be open to the spontaneous moments that make each rehearsal a unique, flexible event?

Worst rehearsal:
Two rehearsals, neither of which I had any control. It was either the manure truck that flipped on the road by the windows during my high school choir's rehearsal, or it was watching one of my singers throw up in front of the choir while we had a guest clinician....no, he was honestly ill.

Dr. Jo-Michael Scheibe
Director of Choral Studies
Frost School of Music, University of Miami

Always treat a rehearsal as something in progress! Rome wasn't built in a day, neither can fine choral organizations. I always enjoy the process more than the destination. Concerts affirm the way we did our job, not becoming the sole reason that we rehearse. Our rehearsals, when well thought out and planned, and when using great vocal/choral modeling, will become much like an adventure. Remember, choral rehearsals are much like a jungle, full of quicksand, swamps, and perilous beasts, but if taken in the right context (the music), we avoid the swamps, the quicksand, and the perils, and find ourselves bridging over these dangers, only to become more aware of the beauty around us. Discovery is everywhere, especially when a dialogue of ideas between conductor and choristers is present.

Some of the best rehearsals that my choristers have experienced is when the conductor has a guided rehearsal process, builds on the golden proportion, and is fully prepared. It is guided by the conductor's innate study of the musical score, guided by intellect, with a considerable amount of heart and soul. The rehearsal must also be free of tension. Tension must be replaced by a sense of playfulness, and must include laughter, and a sense of purpose, community, and ensemble.

Constantina Tsolainou
The Paul S. and Jean R. Amos Faculty Chair in Music and Director of Choral Activities
Schwob School of Music, Columbus State University

Considering how I might describe the perfect rehearsal, I was reminded of my first instructional video and I realized that a portion of that title: "…Language and Style, Principles and Application" pretty much sums it up. If we first establish an approach to sound that is applicable to the piece(s) we are about to rehearse, and if the choir can take that information and apply it as we rehearse, we are well on our way. As a result, the music comes alive and we feel like we have recreated something—as it was intended to be by the composer/arranger. What satisfaction we feel when it is not just the mechanics of music, but the music as a whole that comes alive in a rehearsal. When that happens, we move toward perfection.

Dr. Jing Ling Tam
Professor of Music, Director of Choral Studies
University of Texas at Arlington

It is very difficult to describe the perfect rehearsal because there are so many variables for each rehearsal. It all depends on what you are trying to achieve in a particular setting. It depends on who you are working with, what you are working on, and what goals you have set for the rehearsal. It might be that you are about to step on stage with the New York Philharmonic and are in the final rehearsal or you may be at the first rehearsal for a high school choral festival. These are very different types of experiences. Even when you have set goals yourself, you may find that the goals you have set are not appropriate to the situation once you begin. Even considering this wide variety of possibilities, the key seems to be in setting clear goals for each situation and being able to measure whether those goals were met. Certainly one of the main goals for me in any rehearsal is that the singers or players are fully engaged in the process of music making. When that happens, it gets as close to perfection as one might hope.

Derek Edward Weston
Artistic Director, Una Voce: The Florida Men's Chorale
Director of Choral Studies, Pinellas County Center for the Arts

The best rehearsals always begin before the rehearsal with preparation on the part of the ensemble and the conductor. The greatest music-making experiences in ensembles are the result of a thorough rehearsal plan by the conductor and by score study on the part of ensemble members. This enables both parties to approach rehearsal, and ultimately a performance, with charisma and creates a resulting product that is both musically and artistically excellent.

The worst rehearsals for high school choirs are the ones that begin at 7:00 a.m. when I am barely awake, let alone the teenagers! Not only are the students half-asleep, their vocal folds are not the least bit warm. Once you actually wake up the students and run a thorough warm-up, there is little time for any actual work to be done in rehearsal! As the conductor, I make extraordinary efforts to be as energetic as possible.

Joe Nadeau
Artistic Director, Heartland Men's Chorus, Kansas City

My best rehearsal began like every other rehearsal with stretches, warm-ups, and working on a new piece of music. The only difference was that when I came into rehearsal, I did not say one word. (I worked this out with the accompanist ahead of time.) I spent 20 minutes not speaking at all, which took the chorus off guard and caused them to listen, focus, and wonder what was up. I was forced to use only my gestures to communicate. It was great. When I did speak, I mentioned to the singers that this was the type of focus needed to pull off this music in performance.

My worst rehearsal was with one of my church choirs. I really wanted to sing a certain John Rutter piece that the singers had had in their packets for weeks. It became apparent that the accompanist was struggling with the work and I was hoping by the fifth week that she would have at least tried to work out the rhythms outside of rehearsal. She did not and the piece fell apart, yet again. I was having a bad day anyway, and lost my cool. In a curt and angry voice, I told the singers to give me their music now – this is obviously not going to work. I collected the music and we moved on to another piece, but as I looked at these men and women I saw the look of defeat in their faces. My angry outburst had caused this to happen and the rest of the rehearsal was a disaster. The following Sunday, I apologized for my behavior and expressed that I was venting my frustration on them – something I have never done with any choir since.

Craig Gregory
Executive Director, Tallahassee Community Chorus

- If possible, sing every piece every time you meet (for memorization).
- Lesson Plans are VITAL! It keeps the rehearsal moving.
- The worst chorus members are other choral directors. Engage them in the process.
- Rehearse as you will be in performance when possible.
- Outline and practice your bows in rehearsal: soloists, accompanist, chorus!
- Go with the flow and make 'em laugh!

127

Singers

Doug Clifton

I have had what I consider to be two truly great and highly effective conductors in my 30-year music career, one choral and one band. They share many characteristics, behaviors, and techniques.

Both have a wit that is funny (and occasionally scathing!) that I thoroughly enjoy. The band director could give the best backhanded compliments! Neither would stand for anything less than one's best during rehearsal and knew how to not only draw that out of a group, but also were able to recognize when the group may not be fully focused or just not able to give 100 percent at a particular rehearsal.

Technique Training
I enjoy the "mini-lessons" at the beginnings of rehearsals. It may be like trying to "keep a wave upon the sand," but it keeps me mindful of areas I may have let slide or hone a technique that I have improved in and recognize something more that could be done.

Resolution
As for the rehearsing of music, I dislike not being allowed to complete a phrase or song to its resolution, or not being allowed to finish a piece. I recognize why it is done. It subconsciously keeps us wanting to keep going and sets up anticipation until we finally get to that feeling of resolution/ending/completion. However, we always get through the last song of the evening, thus leaving the rehearsal feeling good, having enjoyed the rehearsal, and looking forward to coming back to the next one. This is a VERY effective rehearsing technique!

Pacing
Pacing is a huge key. It demands that the group pay attention. Keeping the group moving from section to section within a piece or from piece to piece quickly keeps the group on its toes and of course allows us to cover more material during the rehearsal. This keeps the group getting better and more focused.

128

Brow-beating vs. Praise

Limiting "brow-beating" or frustration at the group's lack of progress to critical times is appreciated, only when truly needed. Praise is great. However, sometimes when the praise is too effusive, I feel I don't need to keep pushing as hard as I have been, and sometimes I think the chorus as a whole relaxes some and loses a bit of its momentum. Sometimes I am not sure the praise is actually sincere, but I remind myself that what is heard at the conductors' podium is much different than that of the back rows, which is where I have been for most of my 30 years in music!

Rob Dulaney

I enjoy exercises in rehearsal that provide a challenge, such as a time we formed octets in a circle around the room and took turns singing for each other, one octet at a time. This helped me vocalize as a group, not as a soloist, and built a sense of unity with my baritone brothers. We also heard what the others we don't sit or stand near sound like. Most importantly, the "threat" of this exercise popping up again makes me strive to be better prepared.

Kok-Hong Tan

The worst rehearsal experience I had was my first. I thought singing was a simple task as long as I could carry a tune. After attending my first rehearsal with around 50 singers, I realized that my unfamiliarity with basic music theory made me struggle so much that I was not able to sing what I knew I was supposed to or what I felt. With the feeling of going into an exam hall unprepared, I broke out in cold sweat throughout the entire rehearsal. I later read a saying from a music theory book that rehearsing without the basic knowledge of music is like "an illiterate person going into a library." Just carrying a tune is obviously not enough, but many people don't know that going into the experience.

Jeffrey Mena

I must tell you the best rehearsals for me happen when we sing <u>and</u> spend time forming a family by focusing on how we are feeling about our shared experiences. My best rehearsal came when I was finally able to stand up in a rehearsal and tell my choir family that they had given me a gift I hadn't expected – a real family – and a shared love of singing.

Others

All of the Turtle Creek Chorale rehearsals are open to the public. We have nothing to hide and it keeps me and the singers on their best behavior! As my final season with the chorale began, I met a reporter from a local newspaper who asked if he might chronicle my twentieth season for the paper. I was thrilled. He attended our first rehearsal of the season, which was one for the books. All first rehearsals are a bit chaotic with new music, new people, etc. This one was especially remarkable in that the entire part of the city in which we rehearse experienced a power outage halfway through the rehearsal causing us to simply stop and go home! The second rehearsal of the season was marked by floods at the very minute we began singing, flooding the church where we were rehearsing. We were grateful the third rehearsal was not visited by locusts. Here is the reporter's experience at his first TCC rehearsal.

Richard Lopez
The Dallas Observer

The last thing I expected at a local bookstore was a casual introduction leading to a life-affirming experience. On a Saturday afternoon, I met Dr. Tim Seelig, Artistic Director for the Turtle Creek Chorale in Dallas. He was looking for books on conducting and had his daughter with him. He was gracious, books in hand, while I doted on the Chorale and all that it meant to me to see their performances. So much so that he invited me to the first rehearsal of his twentieth, and final, season with the Turtle Creek Chorale. As a huge fan, this was the equivalent of going backstage to the Rolling Stones concert. Or better yet, Madonna! I would get to watch exactly how my beloved chorale would create the magic that so often moves me to tears and inspires me to be a better man. What should I wear?

On the following Tuesday evening, I made my way to the rehearsal hall. I wasn't sure what to expect but I was immediately in awe of the huge room filled with, I would later find out, some 200 members or potential members of the Chorale. I arrived ten minutes late and the room was almost at capacity with rows of singers prepping with massages and vocal exercises while other latecomers scrambled for a seat so as not to miss any more than they already had. The mass had morphed into something larger and grand. The Chorale's membership runs the gamut of men, from young to old, black to white, mild to wild, but a cohesive tendency brings these numerous individuals into one force of song. And this is just the rehearsal!

The reason Seelig invited me was to observe a rehearsal and, as a reporter, perhaps write something about it. All I could think was, "Doe, a deer, a female deer." Why? Well, years ago, with dreams of multiple Oscars on my mantle, I decided to take up acting. It was my passion that fizzled out after a few years, along with my dreams of having my name on the Hollywood Walk of Fame. But I digress. My first show was a community theater run of "The Sound of Music," hence the deer, and my path to fame began as a Nazi socialite and soldier. An interesting casting choice for one Rich Lopez.

The reason I bring this up is that first rehearsal back then had me in the shakes big time. If there was ever a feeling of anxiety and intimidation, it was walking into a room with what I was certain were all experienced actors and seasoned veterans. I could tell even the darn kids were better than me! As weeks went on, the director convinced me that my ensemble part was just as important as Liesl's. It was a nice try, but it made me feel good. However, that was all I needed and each rehearsal after that was affirming and a step forward.

I had the same feeling of nerves walking into theirs. First, because I was out of my element, but also because potential members were mixed in the crowd. My empathic powers must have been tuned in because I could only think of how these "newbies" might be feeling. By procedure, the Chorale rehearses first and auditions new members soon after. So these new guys had to be good enough to follow along, hold a note and figure if they were tenors, altos or basses. I'm sure previous experience prepared them for such but that was lost on me. The shakes were coming back.

And then they sang. I wasn't sure what these guys were rehearsing for. They sounded amazing! I had to resist the urge of giving a standing ovation of one. But to the untrained ear, mainly mine, I couldn't hear whatever imperfections Seelig heard. With a perfectionist's intensity, he barked out notes and conducted vigorously and they fell into place all working toward the best sound they could produce. At the end of each song, Seelig would make his comments and clap for the good job done.

That's where it hit me.

For those few small moments after each song, I could relate. Me relating to the Turtle Creek Chorale who have been heroes to me for years! I was astounded. As ideal as something may be, it can always be better and the smallest part or the quietest singer is still a thread in a larger quilt. Not only that, I left with a profound impact. Rehearsal just isn't for the stage. Onstage the goal is the performance and when that's done, a sense of pride abounds. But in our everyday life, we rehearse by studying, reading, working out, saving money and whatever else we find we need for the biggest goal we can only hope to achieve – being our best selves and creating a legacy deserving of a standing ovation.

Chris Clarke-Epstein, CSP (Certified Speaking Professional)

Author: *Thinking for a Change*; and
Better Ideas on Leadership, Teamwork, and Feedback for Smart People Who Dare to Make Change Happen

Truly great performances look effortless. All of the work, nervousness, and sweat disappear into the magic of professionals working together. Rehearsals, not so much! Unless, that is, they are run by Dr. Timothy Seelig – then the rehearsal can be magic.

"Great," said my friend Gary Rifkin, "since you'll be in Dallas on Tuesday, you can go with me to Chorale rehearsal." As a longtime admirer of the Turtle Creek Chorale and a lover of all things sung, I felt as though I'd won a backstage pass to the setup rehearsal before a Streisand concert. I could observe, in person, how the magic that is Turtle Creek happens.

Walk into a wonderful space. The home of Turtle Creek, Sammons Center, welcomes you as you enter. Lots of men, rebonding for the evening with hugs, kisses, and good-natured ribbing. High energy, good light, so-so food – it's all about the music. As any leader knows, getting attention and focusing a group at a moment like this can ruin the natural exuberance that has built. In strides, Tim, taking his position in the front of the rehearsal space, tapping the music stand lightly with his conductor's baton, and announcing it's time for a Chorale back rub. Random clusters of men become tenors, baritones, and basses as they form lines and put their hands on their neighbor's shoulders and begin a rhythmic massage. Another few taps with the baton and all eyes focus forward. Chords on the piano establish key and rhythm. Typical warm-up scales are punctuated with physical movement. Energy focused, Turtle Creek is almost ready to sing.

The rest of the rehearsal flows between pieces of songs performed, pieces practiced, and pieces defined; stops and starts to find right notes, interesting rhythm, and perfect emphasis. Laughter flows as easily as beautiful music. In just the right balance, songs are sections to be practiced and whole works to be performed. Time for a break.

I am amazed that the evening is more than half over. The magic of music Seelig-style has taken me out of real time and place. I am back in the rehearsal halls of my past, longing to sing. "Here, Chris," says Gary as he hands me a stack of sheet music. "I bet you can sing the tenor." "Bliss," I think. "Isn't it time for the break to be over?" Clutching the folder, now I'm waiting to hear the baton call us to order. Now we sing. I go from observer to performer, listening to Tim's comments with an increasingly intense perspective. As I sing, my aspirations take on epic proportions. "My hair is short," I muse. "In a tux, standing in the middle of the tenors, I could pass." No matter that my home in Wausau, WI is thousands of miles from Dallas. No matter that no one asked me. No matter that I know none of the music. I am transported to believing in my, no, <u>our</u> ability to perform together. That is, after all, what rehearsals are for.

Tim calls for one more song. "All the way through," he says. "Like it's for real." A collective inhale, music from the piano, and singing. At the end, a hush as the rich music fills the hall. "That, gentlemen, is performance ready." The magic has happened. The rehearsal is over.

Resources

Books

The Perfect Blend
Tim Seelig
Shawnee Press
Nashville, Tennessee

The Musician's Soul
James Jordan
GIA Publications, Inc.
Chicago, Illinois

Conducting Choral Music
Robert L. Garretson
Prentice Hall
Upper Saddle River, New Jersey

Directing the Choral Music Program
Kenneth H. Phillips
Oxford University Press
New York, New York

The Inner Game of Music
Barry Green
Doubleday
New York, New York

The Choral Singer's Survival Guide
Tony Thornton
Vocal Planet
Los Angeles, California

Choral Charisma: Singing with Expression
Tom Carter
Santa Barbara Music Publishing
Santa Barbara, California

Basics of Vocal Pedagogy
Clifton Ware
McGraw Hill
New York, New York

The Art of Conducting
Michael Bowles
Doubleday
Garden City, New Jersey

Introduction to Type in Organizations
A Guide to Understanding Your Results
  on the Myers-Briggs Type Indicator
Consulting Psychologists Press, Inc.
Palo Alto, California

Video/DVDs

The Perfect Blend
Tim Seelig
Shawnee Press

Choral Perspective – Perpetual Inspiration
Weston Noble
Hal Leonard

Choral Perspective – Chant and Beyond
Paul Salamunovich
Hal Leonard

What They See Is What You Get
Rodney Eichenberger with André Thomas
Hinshaw Music

Ensemble Diction
James Jordon/Constantina Tsolainou
Hinshaw Music

Attention to Detail: A Chorale Conductors Guide
Dale Warland
American Choral Catalog

Periodicals

"The Choral Journal"
American Choral Directors Association

"The Voice"
Chorus America

"The Journal of Singing"
National Association of Teachers of Singing

Websites

www.shawneepress.com
www.choralnet.org
www.acdaonline.com
www.chorusamerica.org
www.menc.org
www.galachoruses.org
www.classicalsinger.com
www.nats.org
www.ifcm.net

Who Was Your Guide?

Educator, conductor, singer, speaker, leader, motivator, writer, guide, friend, Dad.

As an educator, Dr. Seelig holds four degrees, including Doctor of Musical Arts from the University of North Texas and the Diploma in Lieder and Oratorio from the Mozarteum in Salzburg, Austria. He has served on the adjunct music faculty at the Meadows School for the Arts at Southern Methodist University since 1996 where he teaches voice and Vocal Pedagogy.

As a conductor, 2007 marks his 20th season as Artistic Director of the Turtle Creek Chorale. Under his leadership, the chorale has continued to stretch the world of male choral music. This season will be his final one as Artistic Director. During his tenure, the chorale grew from a membership of 40 to 350, performing in six separate ensembles. The budget of $69,000 grew to $1.7 million annually. Under his direction, the Turtle Creek Chorale has recorded 37 compact discs, reaching Top 10 on the Billboard classical charts. The Chorale has been the topic of two documentaries, the first of which was awarded an Emmy in 1994. Invited to perform at eight national, regional and state ACDA conventions and for the Eastern Regional MENC convention, the Chorale has also performed across the U.S., including Carnegie Hall, and to sold-out audiences in Barcelona, Prague and Berlin.

Dr. Seelig's early training was as a singer. He made his European operatic debut at the Staatsoper in St. Gallen, Switzerland and his solo recital debut at Carnegie Hall in 1991. He has two solo recordings, *Everthing Possible* and *Two Worlds*. He is a published arranger and lyricist and has contributed to several books on choral technique. His best-selling book, *The Perfect Blend*, was followed by an instructional DVD and *The Perfect Rehearsal*.

Dr. Seelig continues a busy guest conducting schedule with workshop appearances throughout the U.S. and Europe. As a clinician, appearances include state conventions of the American Choral Directors Association in Indiana, New Mexico, Iowa, and Kansas; the national MENC convention as well as state conventions including Texas, Oregon, Indiana, Connecticut, New Hampshire, and Florida; and all-state choirs including South Dakota, Connecticut, Michigan, and Oregon. He serves as the Chairman of the Choral Advisory Committee for the Dallas Independent School District. He has been a recent guest lecturer at Michigan State University, Kansas University, Texas State University, Stetson University, and Vandercook College.

Dr. Seelig has been honored on many occasions. A few of these honors include University of North Texas Distinguished Alumnus, The Dallas Historical Society designation of "history maker of today," and the Dallas Theater Center's "pillar of the Dallas artistic community," as well as carrying the Olympic torch as a community hero. Most recently, Dr. Seelig was awarded the Hero of Hope award for his 20 years of service with the TCC.

He is the proud father of two incredible children.

Reviews

"A good rehearsal begins with a good warm-up and no one explains all the ins and outs better than Timothy Seelig."

The VOICE of Chorus America

"*The Perfect Blend* is a hands-on book that never becomes tedious or overwhelming to read. Seelig's humorous and holistic approach to technique makes this book not only a joy to read, but more importantly, reminds us that we are, after all, teaching the person inside the singer."

AMERICAN MUSIC TEACHER

"Dr. Seelig takes eclecticism to new heights."

GRAMMY MAGAZINE

"Conductor Seelig has raised this group up from the ranks of amateur choir to one receiving wide attention for its excellent performances of appealing, fresh repertoire."

FANFARE MAGAZINE

"As fine a male chorus as I'll ever hope to hear."

AMERICAN RECORD GUIDE

"An accomplished chorale, under Dr. Timothy Seelig, theirs is a joyful noise."

USA TODAY

"Known as a fine singer, he also slices a thick cut of ham."

FORT WORTH STAR TELEGRAM

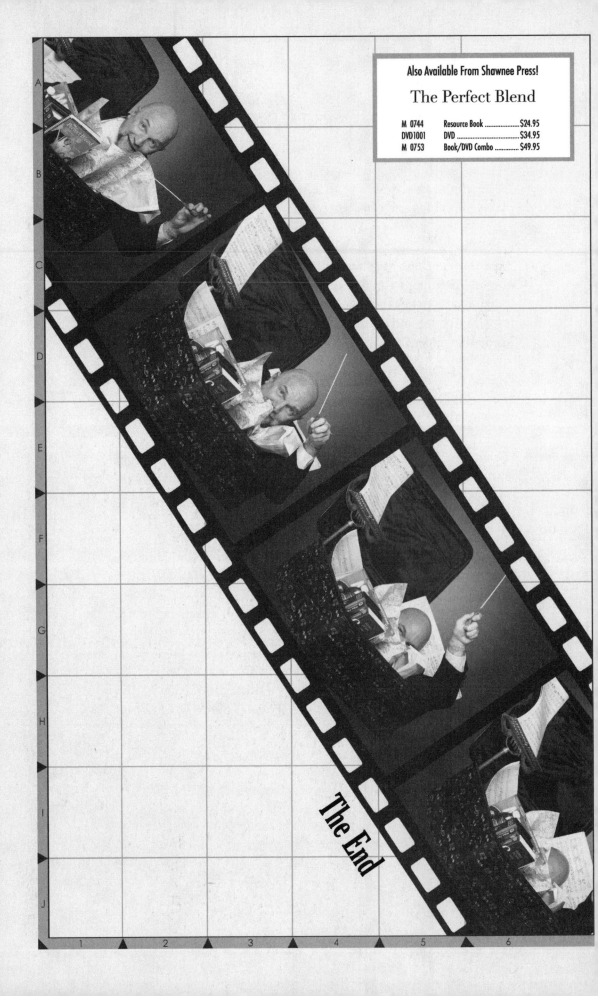

The End